The Quarrymen's Tyddynnod

Dewi Tomos

ISBN: 1-84527-088-6

Cover design: Sian Parri

Published by
Gwasg Carreg Gwalch, 12 Iard yr Orsaf, Llanrwst,
Wales LL26 0EH.
☎ 01492 642031   ▤ 01492 641502
✉ books@carreg-gwalch.co.uk
Web site: www.carreg-gwalch.co.uk

Dedicated to the incomers to our beautiful part of the world, so that they may learn of and appreciate our rich heritage. I would also like to present this work to my Geography teacher at Ysgol Dyffryn Nantlle, Peter Ellis Jones. It was his inspiration and enthusiasm that lit my interest in geographical matters, and it was through field work with him that I first became aware of and proud of my locality. I have a lot to thank him for.

Maps

Thanks

To Dr. Gwynfor Pierce Jones and Dr. Dafydd Gwyn for advice on aspects of quarrying history and archaeology.

To Arwel Jones, Ty'n Rhosgadfan and Arwel Williams, Penffridd for local history.

To Caernarfon Library and Archives staff.

To Dr. Dafydd Glyn Jones for his kind introduction, and his valuable suggestions.

To Anwen Evans for editing the work and to Gwasg Carreg Gwalch for their usual co-operation.

Contents

Introduction

From my little patch of land above Carmel village I can see most of the two parishes of Llandwrog and Llanwnda. Looking north, over Cors Dafarn and the river Llifon valley and towards Moeltryfan's slopes, I can count about forty of Uwchgwyrfai Common's 'tyddynnod', this book's topic. Quite lately I brought to the attention of incomers of neighbours one noted fact about the history of these 'tyddynnod'. 'Look,' I said, 'all freeholdings, as far as I know. When the locality's old families lived in these houses not a penny of rent was paid to neither squire nor landowner. That is something exceptional in the old Caernarvonshire's history and in most of Wales' history. Remember that.' Then I tried to condense for them the famous trouble of 1826, when Lord Newborough's attempts to possess the upper reaches of the two parishes was defeated. A lucky coincidence of events secured that victory; because of that it is not indicative of a trend, and it would be too much to claim any great political significance to it. Yet, as a successful example of 'dal dy dir', 'keep your land', it lifts the spirit and fosters pride – even for me whose family had not reached the locality by then. It would be a great topic for a musical or rock opera.

In reality the 'tyddynnod' have a short history, as this book clearly shows. Only a few are really old, such as Pen Bwlch Bach, Carmel – or Pant y Pwll earlier, as Mona Jones, who was brought up there, showed me. Most were the product of nineteenth century sweat and labour, younger in age and higher on the slopes than the 'Hafodydd' and 'Hafotai' which are in a line about 400-600 feet up across both parishes. (The two obvious exceptions, as far as I can remember, are Hafod at the foot of Mynydd Mawr and Hafod Ruffydd, high on Moeltryfan's north-eastern shoulder.) This study shows such a stunning turn of events the tyddynnod saw within a period of not much more than half a century, from the busy time of their building during the quarries peak till today where there is not much choice but to become ruins or be bought by incomers. It would have been better if someone had shouted 'Dal dy dir!' (hold your land) during the forties and fifties of the twentieth century. But hardly anybody thought so at that time, and here we are by now with a huge problem that nobody really knows the answer to. Maybe the old Welsh peole had part of the answer. I maintain that every Welshman still has a right to a 'hendref' and 'hafod', if his circumstances in any way allow. Let us not be fickle : a holiday home or a second home is all right if it's owned by a Welshman. What about it, our exile children who went to be 'inhabitants of low land and men of fine arts'? It isn't by a long way a complete answer to the problem, but it's one way of 'keeping your land'.

My friend Dewi Tomos (Dewi Hywel, or to be more precise Dewi Hŵal, to us Carmelites) is by now the author of a good number of volumes, most of them inspired by his consuming interest in his locality and his feelings towards it. I place his lecture *Atgof Atgof Gynt*, published in the 'Darlithoedd Llyfrgell Penygroes' series, 1997, amongst the half dozen best within my memory and experience. Dewi is also a man of wide-ranging interests, and from that comes this volume's distinctiveness. There is more to 'the square mile' than reminiscences and personal impressions, precious as they are, and Dewi has applied his knowledge of geology, botany, ecology and economic and social history to provide us with a new look on a familiar world. He chose also to quote liberally from the work of previous authors: this locality has been exceptionally lucky in the writers that came to describe and interpret it, and since several years ago Dewi has joined that illustrious throng of interpretators. I am certain that many, like myself, will take special enjoyment from this book.

Dafydd Glyn Jones

Preface – the Common's hold on me

A line of mountains backs bowed by age,
Watching man's fragility embroidering
In their wounds their region's beauty,
A network above the bracken
Of wires and huge masts,
Filth where was green purity,
Rubble heaps like hunched witches
Their ragged petticoats spoiling the meadows.
Aborted alder and rowan hiding the mountains' scars,
Slate pits under water
As quiet as the cemetries' dead.

'Cadwynnau' (Chains) Tom Huws

Several generations of my family lived on the 'tyddynnod', the smallholdings, on the edges of the common land on the slopes of Mynydd y Cilgwyn, in Pen Carmel, Pencilan, Gogerddan, Tŷ Newydd Cim and Pen-ffynnon-wen. The sons followed their fathers to work in the local quarries, my father and his three brothers, an uncle on my mother's side, my grandfathers and great grandfathers. This succession ended with me when I worked in Moeltryfan Quarry during my college summer holidays.

I was born in Carmel in 1942 and brought up in a village typical of the slate quarrying areas. This was my home until 1965 when I started work in Liverpool, from whence I returned to the area when I got married in 1973 and settled in Rhostryfan. I've lived here with my family ever since and I have no inclination to move. Here I will remain until I 'slip back into the great stillness'. You can therefore see that I've spent most of my life within reach of Uwchgwyrfai Common. We took the common for granted as children in Carmel and made good use of it as a wonderful playground. Mynydd y Cilgwyn was the best place on Earth in those days, and it remains high on the list, along with Moeltryfan and Mynydd Mawr, or Mynydd Grug, 'Heather Mountain', as we called it. These are the mountains that I've climbed more often than any others; this is where I feel completely at home, at one with the world around me, where I get peace of mind. Considering all this, no wonder I have such a close bond with Uwchgwyrfai Common.

I'm not really sure who I am
In rich peat-free lowlands.

The redness of my blood long generations since
Knows there's difference between land and land.

But I know who I am, if I have a hill
A marsh and rushes and rock and lake.

'Cynefin' (Habitat) T H Parry-Williams

What sort of place was it and is it? What changes have occurred? What
will it's future be?

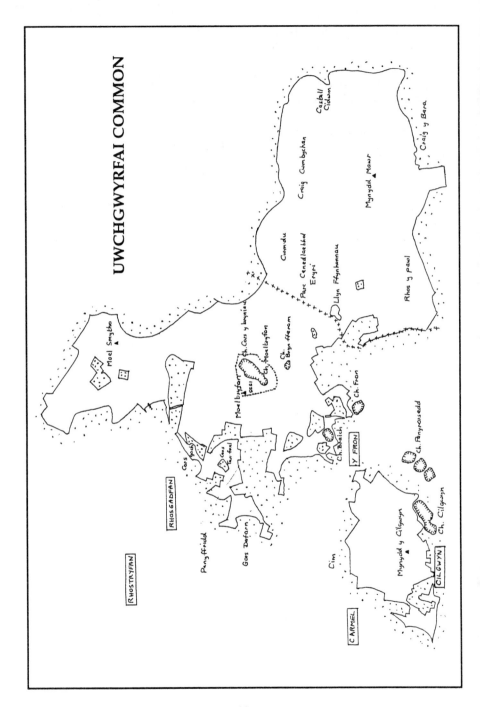

UWCHGWYRFAI COMMON

Site

Uwchgwyrfai Common is situated within the parishes of Llanwnda, Llandwrog and Betws Garmon, about six miles South-west of Caernarfon in Gwynedd. It includes the mountains Mynydd Mawr, Moel Smytho and Mynydd y Cilgwyn, on land between 200 and 700 metres, covering an area of about 2500 acres. It's owned partly by the Crown, partly by the slate quarry owners, and part of it lies within the boundary of Parc Cenedlaethol Eryri National Park. An area around the summit of Moeltryfan is a Site of Special Scientific Interest (SSSI).

It extends from the northern extremity by the mountain wall near Pen-yr-allt (SH 516586) towards the S.W. encompassing the Hafod y Wern forest (523572) onwards towards the Park boundary (529588), westwards up Mynydd Mawr (537549), then east to Craig y Bera (543543) and to Fron (508547), S.E. to Mynydd y Cilgwyn (494548), past Carmel village (493554) and N.W. past the Moeltryfan slate heaps to Rhosgadfan (501576) and then following the mountain wall back to Pen-yr-allt.

Geology

The area's geology includes rocks mainly dating to the Cambrian and Ordovician periods, with some outcrops of igneous rocks. There is a succession of layers on Moeltryfan, from Tryfan grit to Cilgwyn conglomerate to Llanberis slate. In addition there are marine deposits from the period 18 000 years ago when the Irish Sea and Eryri glaciers met. Further glacial evidence is seen on the northern side of Mynydd Mawr and in Cwm Du.

The summit of Moeltryfan was designated an SSSI because of its geological significance. It is described as a classic Pleistocene site of considerable historic importance, with a high level of shell deposits first described by Joshua Trimmer in 1831 in a letter to the geologist William Buckland. The shells were discovered when digging for slate; some were recognised and it was seen that they were of similar type to those on local beaches. It appears that Trimmer was the chief steward at Penyrorsedd Quarry at the time, a keen geologist who was elected a member of the Geological Society in 1832. He published 'Practical Geology and Mineralogy' in 1841, the fruits of his experiences in the quarries most likely.

Many quarrymen, who did not have the advantages of higher education, learnt practical knowledge of the area's geology by experience of trying to locate the best seams of slate. Charles Darwin visited North Wales in 1831 with the eminent geologist Adam Sedgwick, visiting Penrhyn Quarry and Cwm Idwal. In 1842 he returned to Eryri, to Cwm Idwal and Llanberis, and then to Moeltryfan to follow Trimmer's trail. He inspected the summit rocks looking for shell fossils. It's highly likely that I have touched the very same rocks! The local name for them is Barclodiad y Cawr (Devil's apron-full).

This discovery gave rise to one of the fiercest geological debates between the most eminent geologists of the nineteenth century. The crux of the debate was between the Glacialists, who believed in the new Glacial Theory, and the Diluvialists, who believed in the Biblical Flood as the basis of geological features. A strong argument in favour of the Glacial Theory was put forward as a result of studies of drift deposits on Moeltryfan summit and following other studies of prominent glacial features in places like Cwm Idwal. When the two glacial masses met the marine deposits were uplifted to their present height as the seashells in the conglomerate rock prove.

The outcrops of different rocks influenced early settlement, with the variety of rock and ores found on the surface facilitating the building of homes and defences, as well as tool and weapon manufacture. Slate outcropped on Moeltryfan and Cilgwyn, part of the Dyffryn Nantlle seam; iron working evidence was found at Hafoty Wernlas; copper was mined at Drws-y-coed, near the Common's boundary; the remains of iron working in Betws Garmon.

At least four different soils can be found on the Common:

Bangor: a soil consisting of a thin layer of acidic peat over acidic crystalline rock, and as a result of lack of depth it soaks easily, but dries quickly as well, and therefore only remains saturated for about three months, though this has worsened over recent wetter winters. It is mostly heather moorland, with some peat bogs and pools.

Brickfield: on Carboniferous rock, shale or sandstone, it is a clayey soil with slow permeability, and therefore saturated for long periods, even with drainage. Mostly rough pasture with an abundance of rushes.

Hexworthy: a podzolic soil, on Moeltryfan over rhyolite. It consists of rocky ground with scattered boulders and stony soil with little depth. It is mainly open, heathery moorland with marsh vegetation in the wettest areas.

Manod: a mainly clayey soil with good drainage over slate or Palaeosoic mudstone, mostly on sloping ground, which combined with the heavy rainfall (+1000mm. p.a.) means most nutrients are washed away resulting in acidic soil, low in phosphorus. The base rock is very near the surface in places. Rough pasture or permanent grasses mostly.

Climate

Like the rest of British uplands, Uwchgwyrfai is an area of high rainfall and strong winds, a climate that affects the bio-diversity.

Climatic averages:

Month	Air temperature(C)	Rainfall (mm)	Sunshine (hours/day)
January	2.6	195	1.1
February	2.6	125	2.0
March	4.6	119	3.3
April	6.6	112	4.5
May	9.5	111	5.3
June	12.4	109	5.7
July	13.7	115	4.7
August	13.7	157	4.5
September	12.1	178	3.5
October	9.2	192	2.4
November	5.6	205	1.4
December	3.8	211	1.0

Total 1829
Growing season – 225 days

The locality is within 3-6 miles from the sea with open windswept slopes, the prevailing winds being westerly or northwesterly. Heavy clouds from over the Irish Sea come into contact with the hillsides consequently bringing rain, more rain, mist, and strong winds, but yet a pleasant place to live in!

In the locality of Moel y Fantro, spring comes late and winter early. The lower parish fields would be green before Moel y Fantro fields shed their winter clothes. The latter's trees would be bare when in other places they would wear autumn's clothes. When the wind blew from the sea, Moel y Fantro would be in the teeth of the storm, and the women would have difficulty washing brine from their windows.

Nevertheless, there was a beauty that wouldn't normally be seen.

Every night of their lives the quarrymen saw the sun set over the Irish Sea or over Ynys Môn. In summer, its fire turning Menai to blood for a while, and in winter, its pale, yellow glow ending suddenly. These people saw the September full moon rising over Yr Wyddfa, casting its light over the harvesters. Yet it is questionable whether they took time to appreciate the scenery at all.

Yr Athronydd, 'O Gors y Bryniau', Kate Roberts

Moel y Fantro was Moeltryfan. I also saw from the Carmel of my childhood, and I can see from my home in Rhostryfan, the wondrous sunsets turning Yr Eifl to Vesuvius in December, outlining the Wicklow Mountains in Ireland, laying a magic red carpet over the Foryd.

Landscape

The common's landscape is typical of the effects of glaciation, undulating, wet ground full of depressions, hillocks and hills. A number of streams, pools and marshes dot the area, including the sources of a number of rivers – Carrog, Wyled, Llifon and their tributaries. The biggest lake by far, Llyn Ffynhonnau, nestles by the foot of Mynydd Mawr. There are several marshes, Cors Dafarn, Cors Tan-foel, Cors Goch and a long one at the foot of Mynydd Mawr. The three lowest mountains, Moel Smytho (243m.), Moeltryfan (427m.), and Mynydd y Cilgwyn (347m.), are rounded, with soil covering mostly and scattered groups of boulders and more prominent rocks on the summit of Moeltryfan. Mynydd Mawr is the highest by far (698m.), also rounded in shape but with steep rock sides and scree to the south, Craig y Bera, and to the north, Cwm Du and Castell Cidwm.

The common and surrounding land forms a landscape not overly spoilt, with low levels of human interference except for the slate quarries and 'tyddynnod', and consequently it is of special environmental interest. The area includes a significant number of archaeological sites and historical remains – some at least 2000 years old. This was the inspiration that O. M. Edwards had on Mynydd y Cilgwyn's summit:

> . . . I then started up the mountain's short grass . . . Whoever can drink mountain inspiration, well then, stand on Carmel's summit. There you see them, a half-spiritual host, from the Eifl to Mynydd Mawr. Yr Wyddfa looking down in majestic modesty through Drws-y-coed. By the mountain's feet, on one side Dinas Dinlle and the sea; on the other side the Nantlle lakes, Penygroes and the mountains.
>
> This is the place to see mountain majesty and the ways of the sea. We are as if in the presence of freedom . . .
>
> *Yn y Wlad* O. M. Edwards

Many of the tyddynnod's names are suggestive of the landscape, Bryn Crin, Manllwyd, Gors Goch, Bryn Gwynt, Hafod y Rhos, Ty'n y Fawnog, Ffridd Lwyd, Bryn Rhedyn and Glan Gors.

The Environment

A variety of habitats can be found within the common, from marginal land near the villages to more remote mountain land on Mynydd Mawr, forming beautiful and dramatic scenery. The habitats vary as a result of the landscape variety. Moeltryfan and Cilgwyn are typical of grassy mountain pasture where Purple moor-grass *(Molinia caerulea)*, Heath rush *(Juncus squarrosus)* and Mat grass *(Nardus stricta)* are commoner than heather, though these plants are often found intermingled with heather species like Cross-leaved heath *(Erica tetralix)* and Bell heather *(Erica cinerea)*.

Within the grassland are patches of heather *(Calluna vulgaris)*, bilberry *(Vaccinium myrtillus)*, mountain crowberry *(Empetrum nigrum)*, rush and bracken, forming a multi-coloured patchwork. The presence of present day vegetation is the result of centuries of grazing by farm animals – mostly sheep for some time, but in the past mainly cattle, with some goats and ponies as well.

By grazing and trampling they discouraged the growth of trees and shrubs, and this is what forms the variety of suitable conditions for flora and fauna. The grazing animals leave droppings, wool, fur and carcasses, which in turn provide a food source for flies, that attract birds such as chough, and the grasses of different heights harbour lapwing and wagtail.

Several detailed ecological surveys have been made by various bodies between 1985 and1989 and by Aberystwyth University Rural Surveys in 1991. There follows a précis of their findings.

A considerable acreage of montane Heath-grass *(Danthonia decumbens)* rich in lichen is found on Mynydd Mawr summit, at a lower altitude than elsewhere in Eryri. It includes short, lichen rich Sheep's fescue (Festuca ovinis), with plenty of recumbent Bilberry and Cowberry *(Vaccinium vitis-idaea)*, and scattered clusters of Crowberry *(Empetrum nigrum)*. Lower plants such as Alpine clubmoss *(Diphasiastrum alpinum)* and Fir clubmoss *(Huperzia selago)* are also found.

Extensive patches of heather moorland are found on Mynydd Mawr and Moel Smytho, a fairly rare habitat in Eryri. Brittle Bladder-fern *(Cystopteris fragilis)*, Beech fern *(Phegopteris conectilis)* and Golden saxifrage *(Saxifraga stellaris)* are found on the rocky northern side of Mynydd Mawr. Great wood-rush *(Luzula sylvatica)* can be seen amongst the bracken in two hollows in Cwm Du, and below them extensive scree including a few Parsley fern *(Cryptogramma crispa)* and some heather. Brittle Bladder-fern *(Cystopteris fragilis)* grows in an old level on Craig Cwmbychan, and on lower wet, acidic land there is Bog asphodel *(Narthecium ossifragum)* and Common butterwort *(Pinguicula vulgaris)*.

Because most of the land is short grass and heather, with numerous pools and marshes, as well as old quarry pits, rubble heaps and old quarry buildings and ruins, and Cilgwyn refuse dump, plenty of variety of bird food is available. There have been several surveys of birds found on the common.

Species of Birds between 1985 and 2000

Butei buteo	*Boda*	Buzzard
Pyrrhocorax pyrrhocorax	*Brân goesgoch*	Chough
Numenius arquata	*Gylfinir*	Curlew
Motacila cinerea	*Siglen lwyd*	Grey wagtail
Circus cyaneus	*Bod tinwen*	Hen harrier
Ardea cinerea	*Crëyr glas*	Heron
Larus argentatus	*Gwylan y penwaig*	Herring gull
Falco tinunculus	*Cudyll coch*	Kestrel
Vanellus vanellus	*Cornchwiglen*	Lapwing
Anas platyrhynchos	*Hwyaden wyllt*	Mallard
Anthus pratensis	*Corhedydd y waun*	Meadow pipit
Falco peregrinus	*Hebog tramor*	Peregrine falcon
Motacilla alba	*Siglen fraith*	Pied wagtail
Corvus corax	*Cigfran*	Raven
Lagopus lagopus	*Grugiar*	Red grouse
Turdus torquatus	*Mwyalchen y mynydd*	Ring ousel
Tringa glareola	*Pibydd y dorlan*	Sandpiper
Alauda arvensis	*Ehedydd*	Skylark
Gallinago gallinago	*Gïach*	Snipe
Saxicola torquata	*Clochdar y cerrig*	Stonechat
Oenanthe oenanthe	*Tinwen y garn*	Wheatear
Troglodytes troglodytes	*Dryw*	Wren

(UW Aberystwyth & Bangor, WFU, RSPB)

There has been a decline in the numbers of some species (e.g. Chough went from 10 pairs in 1985 to one pair in 2000). There was also a dramatic decline in lapwing and curlew numbers on the common and surrounding land. They were frequently seen twenty years ago, I knew of pastures where I would be likely to see half a dozen or more lapwing and I would hear the curlew almost daily from my garden, but not in recent years. I still see the curlew occasionally but not the lapwing where they used to be, though a few are seen on wet pasture in Rhos-Isaf. The decline could be because of dumping rubbish, noise pollution by motorbikes and 4WD vehicles on the common, pollution of fields, more birds of prey like the buzzard, and a change in the intensity of grazing. I haven't seen grouse for a while either, they used to rise from the heather on Moel Smytho quite often twenty years ago. Which is the commonest bird on the common nowadays? Without a shadow of doubt the hundreds of gulls around Cilgwyn dump.

The most common animals are rabbits on the slate tips, an occasional hare S.E. of Mynydd Mawr, goats on Castell Cidwm crags and frogs in the numerous pools. Many a time I collected frogspawn with my children!

A number of sites have been studied as possible Non-statutory Wildlife Sites by the North Wales Wildlife Trust, part of a Gwynedd survey to note important sites to safeguard the bio-diversity, and it's possible that several habitats within the common will be included.

The idle quarries and tips, some over a century old, are slowly but surely being covered by vegetation.

We did not go towards the quarries often, especially us girls. I would be afraid to look down to the bottom of the pit. But there in the rubble heaps we discovered the fern called mountain fern or quarry fern – parsley fern in English. We doted on it, and attempted to grow it at home but nobody succeeded in growing it, the blue slate was its shelter and refuge.

Y Lôn Wen, Kate Roberts

And this is a description of Lôn Wen and Moel Smytho.

They reached the cart track that led to the mountain . . . the road was narrow and hard underfoot. On either side grew heather and gorse, damp moss and peat bogs. The gorse was small and supple, it's flowers the palest yellow like primroses, and the short heather contrasted with it and the dark land around. Little streams ran down from the mountain to the road and the crystal clear water flowed on over the gravely sides. Sometimes the stream ran into a pool and stayed so. Sheep tracks criss-crossed everywhere, and mountain sheep and long tailed ponies grazed on it. Everything connected to the mountain was stunted – the gorse, the moss, the sheep, the ponies.

Traed Mewn Cyffion, Kate Roberts

A number of young trees, mainly rowan and holly, have grown up to three or four feet on the northern side of Mynydd y Cilgwyn. They generally grow out of thick patches of gorse. Why this development? Fewer sheep grazing, less burning of heather and gorse, and so young trees can germinate and grow probably. A widespread fire during the hot dry spring of 2003 did not damage most of them.

It is evident therefore that Uwchgwyrfai common consists of a variety of valuable habitats. Acidic grassland and heather typical of uplands, and in a British context, they are considered of international importance. It is imperative that this diversity is conserved and protected for future generations. The habitats should be conserved and further surveys undertaken to obtain a complete picture, and to try and understand why the numbers of some birds is declining and to ascertain what improvements need to be made. An agreement between agricultural needs, wildlife and landscape conservation is vital, with a clear strategy to defend this valuable piece of land.

Early History (pre 1750):
Iron Age and Middle Ages

Quite often there is no definite boundary between heritage features and we should look at archaeological evidence in its entirety and not at individual sites. The common's present boundary is relatively recent, and so residents of several sites, which now are below the boundary, would have made use of the common land. Evidence shows that there is a concentration of human activities in the area to the S.W. and S.E. of the common and in the region that today contains the 'tyddynnod'.

Oak, hazel, birch, hawthorn and blackthorn grew from sea level to around 600 metres, with alder and deep marshes on the valley floors. Settlements were established on the slopes where the tree covering was not so dense, and so being more conducive to clearing for grazing. Most traces of Iron Age settlements are found in a long belt between 150 – 300m. above sea level, clusters of huts and small fields, here and there amongst the trees. There is evidence that barley was grown and reaped with a scythe or sickle. The fields were often long, sloping strips. They kept cattle similar to the Celtic Shorthorn, sheep like the Soay breed, pigs, ponies and dogs to hunt and shepherd. Wild animals such as wolves, bears, or wild cats could be a danger to the farm animals, and boars and deer were hunted. One of the chief feasts was *Samain*, All Saints'Day, when the stock was gathered, some being kept over winter for breeding and the others killed and their meat salted for winter use. At *Beltaine*, May Day, the stock was sent out to graze after being driven through fire to cleanse them. They had a similar practice to the latter transhumance really.

The lower slopes of Moeltryfan and Cilgwyn, on the 'hafotai's' land, are dotted with prehistoric remains, huts and fields, especially south and north of Rhostryfan.

There are also sites on Mynydd Mawr near Llyn Ffynhonnau, Caeronwy and Gelli. It is one of the best regions in Wales for prehistoric remains, both in number and condition. Gwynedd Archaeological Trust has denoted over forty sites on the common and a number of important sites on 'tyddynnod' land.

Archaeologoical Sites:

1.	Pentre
2. and 3.	Ffynnon Garmon enclosure
4.	probable 16c. chapel E of Ff. Garmon
5.	Ff.G. sheepfold
6.	Moel Smytho
7.	Long hut
8.	hafod, SW of Tŷ Coch
9.	Tŷ Coch dwelling
10.	Alexandra
11.	radiocarbon date, Moeltryfan
12.	Moeltryfan
13.	Bryn Fferam
14.	Crown
15.	Braich
16.	field system & settlement, Maes Hyfryd, Carmel
17.	quernstone, Bryn Brith, Carmel
18.	hut group, Bryn Brith
19. and 20	burnt mound, NE of Cae Forgan, Carmel
21. 22. and 23.	long hut, W Cae Forgan
24.	cairn, Bedd Twrog (unlocated), Cilgwyn
25.	cairn, Cilgwyn
26.	chambered tomb(unlocated), M. y Cilgwyn
27.	hut circles, NE of Gelli Ffrydiau, Nantlle
28.	hut group, SE of Castell Caeronwy
29.	platform hut, SE " "
30.	cairn, Mynydd Mawr summit
31.	platform house, NE of Brithdir Mawr
32. and 33	Castell Cidwm natural feature
34.	cairn, Craig Cwm Bychan
35.	trial levels, Craig Cwm Du
36. and 37	Cwm Du
38.	post-medieval house & paddocks
39.	Cwm Du sheepfold
40.	Cwm Du level
41.	Pen-y-gaer level

(GAT, numbers as on Map 2, page 23)

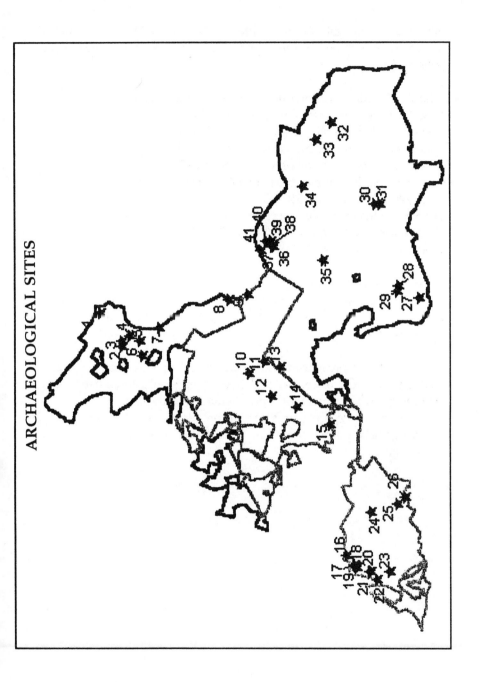

ARCHAEOLOGICAL SITES

There are a number of other sites on neighbouring land, especially between 200-300m to the north and N.W. near Rhosgadfan and Rhostryfan.

Hafoty Wernlas – round enclosures, huts and fields (SH 501582)
Coed-y-brain – cluster of huts (SH 493572)
Hafoty Tŷ Newydd – enclosed huts (SH 497571)
Gaerwen – cluster of huts (SH 500582)
Cae-hen – cluster of enclosed huts (SH 501585)
Pen-bryn-bach – cluster of enclosed huts (SH 511584)
Pen-y-bryn – huts (SH 510585)
Yr Erw – cluster of huts (SH 506589)
Cae'rodyn – huts and fields (SH 495573)
Bodgarad – huts (SH 503583)

In the vicinity of Fron:
Castell Caeronwy – enclosed huts.
Artefacts dating to the Iron Age and Middle Ages around Castell Caeronwy.

Because of the presence of so many Iron Age settlements it is likely that a great deal of the natural tree cover would have been cleared then, for roofing, fuel, tools and to create grazing land.

One can sense some presence, some perpetual continuation, when walking these paths where our forefathers toiled two millennia and more ago.

Transhumance – Hendrefau and Hafotai

During the Middle Ages the main use of the land encompassed by the common today would have been for stock grazing. Comparatively few sheep were kept then, apart from the monasteries, but many cattle were kept, and they would have two homes, the Hendre, winter dwelling or home farm, over the winter months, and the Hafod or Meifod, summer dwelling, during the summer (compare Meifod to *Beltaine*). The cattle were moved on May Day, being marked as sheep are today, so that they could be recognised on the open mountain pastures. So we had the low level farm, the hendref, where crops were grown, and then the hafod on higher pasture.

We find clear evidence of this practice in place names in the vicinity of Carmel and Rhostryfan, Wernlas and Hafoty Wernlas, Pen-y-bryn and Hafoty Pen-bryn, Hafoty Newydd, Hafoty Wen, Hafod Lwyfog, Hafod Talog. Note that the hafotai are on lower ground than the later tyddynnod, originally the hafod would border on the open common. The clearing of trees to create more pasture, for fuel, fencing and building, would have continued during this period.

The lower farms of Llanwnda and Llandwrog parishes were formed into units similar to the present day farms over four centuries ago, middle sixteenth century. This state persisted until about 1750, when a dramatic change occurred.

> . . . the land above the low-lying tilled land was rough open country, and was so to the mountain tops, much of it being marshy moorland, but with a good share of rough, hard pasture, fairly bare, but capable of being improved and turned into land that could be enclosed as small tyddynnod . . . and this was the rough land between 700 and 900 feet above sea level that was settled by the early tyddynwyr along the Welsh foothills, where there was industry, lead, slate and coal . . . It was an especial development in the neighbourhoods of Bethesda, Llanberis and Nantlle, the Arfon slate quarrying areas.
>
> *Y Chwarelwr Dyddynnwr yn Nyffryn Nantlle*, Dr R Alun Roberts

The transhumance way came to an end with the Commons Enclosures. The hafotai became hill farms and there came a noticeable change from keeping cattle to sheep, which were easier to keep on poorer soil over winter.

Relatives of the hendrefau families continued to live on the hafotai near Rhostryfan until the 1830s at least, which suggests that the order persisted until the nineteenth century. e.g. Wernlas Ddu sons in Hafoty Wernlas, Pen-y-bryn family in Hafoty-Pen-bryn, and Tŷ Newydd family in Hafoty Tŷ Newydd.

Folk Stories

Several folk stories are associated with the common, dating back to the transhumance society. Here follows a few short examples:

Castell Cidwm

It is told that Cidwm, Macsen Wledig and Elen Luyddawg's son, hid on the rock above Llyn Cwellyn intending to kill his brother as he passed by with the Roman soldiers. As Cidwm rose to aim his arrow he was spotted by one of the soldiers who shouted, 'Llech yr olaf', (the last man to hide) which thwarted Cidwm's intention. The rock is still called Castell Cidwm, as well as the restaurant by the lake, and there used to be a cottage called 'Llech yr olaf' nearby.

Rhos y Pawl

A farmhand from Gelli fell in love with Talymignedd's daughter but her father refused to give his permission for them to marry. After becoming fed up with the lad's pleading, the father gave him a condition, he could marry his daughter, if he stayed out overnight on the open pasture, stark naked, and this being January. The wily farmer thought that the lad would be too scared to attempt the task, or that if he was foolish enough to do so, then he would surely die of exposure. But the lad hit upon a splendid plan, he took a long pole and a heavy sledgehammer with him to the mountainside. He kept himself from freezing by hitting the pole into the hard ground and resting his head on the warm pole alternatively all through the night. He succeeded, and the young lovers were married. The pasture between Gelliffrydiau and Llyn Ffynhonnau is still called Rhos y Pawl. (pawl = polyn, pole)

Gwas y Gelli

Remote places, and especially mountain lakes, were often associated with the fairies. Once a farmhand from Gelli, another one, went up towards Llyn Ffynhonnau to shepherd. As he came within sight of the lake he saw a group of Little People dancing merrily. He went towards them and was enticed into the dance circle. The shepherd and his poor dog danced away for three whole days non-stop. Luckily for them an old man happened to pass by and he reached into the circle with his rowan stick and managed to pull the lad out of the fairies' clutches.

Industry (since 1750): The Slate Quarries

The situation pre 1750

There would have been intermittent digging for slate on Cilgwyn's slopes, but the main use of the common would have been agricultural, with cattle mainly, and sheep, ponies and a few goats grazing on it. Lowland farmers would come up to dig peat. An area of scarce population therefore, with lowland farms, hafotai, on the pastureland and the common reaching much further down than today.

The growth of the slate industry was a vital factor in the formation of the present-day landscape. A line of quarries was opened from Moeltryfan to Cilgwyn, and the band continues S.E. to Dyffryn Nantlle. There is evidence of surface extraction of slate as early as the Roman occupation at Segontium, with further evidence that Tŷ Mawr, Nantlle had a slate roof when Edward 1 stayed there in 1284. It was intermittent, extracting rock from near the surface only. Small quarries were opened occasionally, to supply local demand, and slates were sometimes carried down to Foryd, and later to Caernarfon for export either to English towns or to Ireland. There was only occasional mining, with no special tools, no permanent employment, or capital invested. By no means could it be classified as an industry at that time.

As a consequence of the Industrial Revolution, by the eighteenth century the rapid growth of towns and cities in Britain meant there was a growing demand for roofing material. Previously there was no transport or proper order to the mining, but now the quarrymen expanded their horizons. Caernarfon was only six miles from Cilgwyn, and though the tracks were rough, slate could be carried on sledges or on horseback.

The real beginning of the slate industry dates to the period from 1750 to 1800 when individual quarrymen united in co-operative ventures, starting to dig in earnest into the ground to find good slate. The development of order and material gain for the quarrymen was very slow though.

A grim light is thrown on conditions in these seemingly flourishing regions by the part quarrymen played in the recurrent food riots at Caernarvon in the middle years of the century. In 1752 a mob of quarrymen from Cilgwyn and Rhostryfan swarmed into the town to raid the granaries there, and in the ensuing armed scuffle with the authorities two men were killed ... Hunger was never far below the surface while agriculture and industry remained undeveloped; and they could never develop so long as the local gentry most capable of infusing capital and enterprise into them diverted these into other channels.

A History of Caernarvonshire, A H Dodd

The nineteenth century was a period of rapid expansion for the industry, with a subsequent major increase in population. Nearly four times as many people lived in the parishes of Llanwnda, Llandwrog and Llanllyfni in 1891 compared with 1801. A terrific increase, that transformed a rural, agricultural, scarcely populated region, into an industrial, highly populated region within a short space of time. But the rural, agricultural aspect was not completely lost, as was usually the case following industrialisation, a special factor belonging to the slate quarrying areas, and a factor that played a vital part in forming the unique character of the society. Because of this dualism between heavy industry and the attachment to rural life, the in-migration from nearby areas to start off, the growth of numerous villages rather than one large town, there was no Anglicisation here as was the case in most areas of heavy industry.

Population of Parishes 1801-1991:

Parish	1801	1851	1891	1971	1991
Llanwnda	826	1607	1954	1655	1855
Lanllyfni	812	2010	4968	3635	4137
Llandwrog	1175	2823	3180	2325	2456
Total	2813	6440	10102	7615	8448

Llechi Lleu, D Tomos & 1991 Census

The following were the principal quarries within, or bounding on, the common:

Uwchgwyrfai Common Quarries

Quarry	Opened	Number Employed
Moeltryfan	circa 1809	81 (1882)
Alexandra	circa 1862	140 (1870)
Y Fron	circa 1810	80 (1873)
Braich	circa 1830	140 (1873)
Cilgwyn	circa 1700	300 (1882)
Pen-yr-orsedd	circa 1816	442 (1892)

A History of the North Wales Slate Industry, Jean Lindsay

I only include brief notes about the quarries as plenty has already been written about them. Sufficient for our study of the common is to note their existence and their effect on the common and surrounding area.

Alexandra or Cors y Bryniau (SH 519569)

On the eastern side of Moeltryfan. A company was formed in 1862 with £15,000 capital, employing 140 workers. Annual produce in 1874 was 6000 tons, and a new company was formed. The Amalgamated Slate Association took over in 1918, and the Caernarvonshire Crown Slate Quarries in 1932. The quarry closed in 1934 but later working from Moeltryfan to Twll Mawr Gors amalgamated them.

Braich (SH 509559)

On the S.W. shoulder of Moeltryfan. Mining began in 1833, re-opened in 1860 by a private company, and by 1873 employed 140. The quarry was one big pit on three levels, and slate was transported on a railroad laid besides Cilgwyn Quarry, before the 1877 Bryngwyn Line. Working ceased about 1914, when the Cors y Bryniau Company worked it.

Cilgwyn (SH 498538)

On the S.E. side of Mynydd y Cilgwyn. Alleged to be the oldest quarry in Wales, dating back to the twelfth century! John Wynn of Glynllifon obtained a 31-year lease for the quarry from the Crown in 1745, but he did not interfere much with the indigenous quarrymen, apart from raising a 4d. p.a. surtax on them. The *Cefn Du Slate Co.* (John Evans,

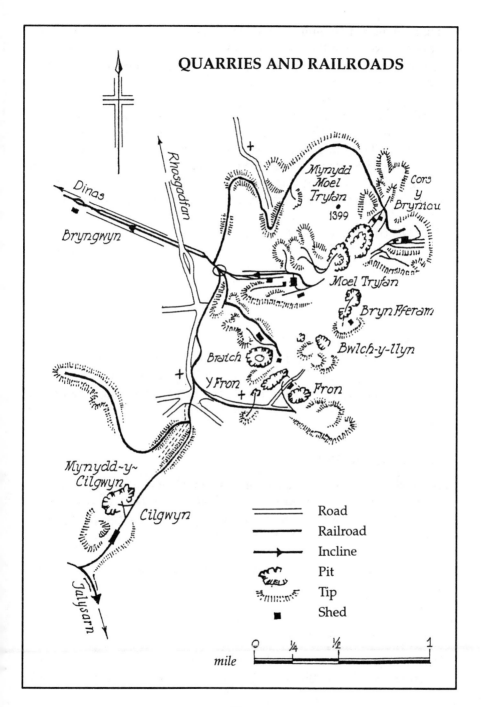

QUARRIES AND RAILROADS

Dinas

Rhosgadfan

Bryngwyn

Mynydd Moel Tryfan
1399

Cors y Bryniau

Moel Tryfan

Bryn Fferam

Bwlch-y-llyn

Braich

y Fron

Fron

Mynydd-y-Cilgwyn

Cilgwyn

Talysarn

Road
Railroad
Incline
Pit
Tip
Shed

O   ¼   ½   1

mile

31

attorney, Caernarfon) took over the lease in 1800 and there ensued fifteen years of conflict between him and the quarrymen before John Evans eventually had his way. From 1835 to 1845 it was owned by a Mr. Muskett, who became bankrupt after overspending on building and equipment. He built Plas y Cilgwyn, which was plundered by the workers in recompense for lack of wages for months. The quarrymen continued working the quarry without the Crown's permission, they thought within their rights, but eventually seven were imprisoned. *Hayward & Co.* from Oswestry took over in 1849, and remained in charge until 1918 when Cilgwyn, Foel and Gors quarries were united by the *Amalgamated Slate Association Ltd.* from Caernarfon. The quarry shut in 1930 till in 1932 it was worked by the *Caernarvonshire Crown Slate Quarries Ltd.* (Owen Owens, Talmaes, J.J. Riley & Lancaster). The quarry shut in 1958 but some scavenging on the tips and buildings mainly for dampcourse continued until 1964-65. There were four pits, Faengoch, Hen Gilgwyn, Cloddfa'r Dŵr and Cloddfa Glytiau.

Fron (SH 514549)

Between Moeltryfan and Cilgwyn, S.E. of Braich. Opened about 1830, re-opened 1860. Produce 1500 tons in 1860, employing 80 in 1873. An incline to Cilgwyn railroad to transport slate to Nantlle railroad, but not used after 1881. Joined with Hen Fraich in 1868, employed 62 in 1882. Worked by O.J. Hughes & Son in 1937, employing seven. Shut 1950.

Moeltryfan (SH 518567)

Alongside Cors y Bryniau quarry. Opened about 1800 by Mesach Roberts under a crown lease to John Evans & Partners. It was worked on a small scale for the next seventy years, for a while jointly with Cloddfa'r Lôn and Penbryn, Nantlle. A local company from Caernarfon ran the quarry from 1876 to 1918 when it became part of the *Amalgamated Slate Co.* and in 1932 the *Caernarvonshire Crown Slate Quarries Ltd.* took over. Twelve men were employed when work ceased in 1972.

Pen-yr-orsedd (SH 505540)

Below Cilgwyn Quarry on the lower slopes of Mynydd y Cilgwyn. Opened 1816 by William Turner, with a capital of £20,000. Heavy spending without any tangible results for a while, but in 1882 produced 7999 tons and employed 261, by 1892 it had 445 workers and the company was noted for its care of the workforce. Produce 3431 tons in 1945-6 and in 1972 employed 20. Bought by Cwmni Llechi Ffestiniog (T.Glyn Williams) in 1979, who sold it in 1979 following a heavy rock fall. Owned presently by McAlpine, with four men extracting green slate, which is sent to Penrhyn Quarry to be processed.

There are plans afoot (2005) by the *Caernarvon Crown Slate Quarries Co.* to re-open Moeltryfan and Cors y Bryniau on a small scale, mainly for ornamental slate.

The industry was at its height by 1886 as the following statistics show:

Quarry	Produce	Number employed 1886
Pen-yr-orsedd	£14800	390
Cilgwyn	£21000	318
Fron	3000	8
Moeltryfan	7400	150
Alexandra	16900	230
Bryn Fferam	nil	2
Total	**£63100**	**1198**

Chwareli Dyffryn Nantlle a Chymdogaeth Moeltryfan, John Griffith, 1889

£63000 was an enormous sum in 1886, and in addition to the 1200 employed here, consider the numerous other quarries in Dyffryn Nantlle. These quarries within the valley were within reach of our area's workforce, and we know that many travelled considerable distances to their workplace from their tyddynnod and villages.

From now on I will depend a great deal on the recollections of eminent writers brought up on the tyddynnod, and especially Kate Roberts – recollections that encompass a period from the second half of the nineteenth century to the first quarter of the twentieth. What better means is there to learn about a period in a locality's history than to read eyewitnesses' memories, and better still if they are amongst our best literary people?

Kate Roberts' grandfather, father and uncle worked in Cilgwyn Quarry, nearly three miles from their homes in Bryn Ffynnon and Cae'r Gors, though there were other quarries on Moeltryfan much nearer. Six miles walking daily, six days a week, as well as chores on the tyddyn!

He had no schooling after turning nine years old . . . But next morning at sunrise, my father set out for Cilgwyn with his brother who was two years older, and his father. He made that journey for nigh on half a century.

Y Lôn Wen, Kate Roberts

Her father would have begun working in Cilgwyn in 1860, staying there till 1907. While reminiscing in *Y Lôn Wen* Kate Roberts remarks that she came across a black-edged memorial card, called a 'mourning card' and written on it:

Er parchus goffadwriaeth
am
ROBERT OWEN ROBERTS
Bryn Ffynnon, Rhos Cadfan,
Yr hwn a fu farw
(trwy ddamwain)
Rhagfyr 23ain, 1861
Oed, 12 mlwydd

Profwyd doethineb rhyfedd – Duw Iôn mawr
Yn myn'd a'n mab hoyw-wedd;
Am fis bron mewn gogonedd –
Cantor fu, cyn torri'i fedd.

Dewi Arfon

(In loving memory of ROR who died by accident,
December 23rd 1861, age, 12 years)

I remember that this card was framed, with a picture of the twelve years old boy underneath it, and hanging on the partition of my old home at one time.

Many a time we heard about this accident at home, from my grandmother and grandfather. My father, though he was only ten years old, had been working in the quarry for a year. The night before the accident, a Sunday night, my father and his brother went out, to the cowshed or somewhere, my father accompanied his brother because it was so dark, when suddenly they heard some big bird screeching overhead. The screech was so unearthly it scared them, and after returning to the house, Robert told his mother that he wasn't going to the quarry the next morning, because of the screeching he'd heard. He was working down the pit, in spite of his youth, when a large fall of rock came down and buried him underneath. It took a month to find his body, which explains the line in Dewi Arfon's englyn *'Am fis bron mewn gogonedd.'* (for nearly a month in glory) It was learnt later that the reason for this was that a blast of wind following the fall had thrown the boy several yards from where he stood, while they searched for him there, and doubtless throwing more rock on top of him. Years later, well after clearing the fall, my grandfather found Robert's clog.

Y Lôn Wen, Kate Roberts

That last sentence is on a slate fence at the Gwerin y Graith site in Parc Glynllifon, a site to remember the writers of the slate quarrying areas. Robert was buried in Horeb cemetery, Rhostryfan. I wonder if it was an owl, ('aderyn corff'- corpse bird), that they heard? Just imagine his father and brother having to work there with his body still buried under the rubble. I took some Cymdeithas Edward Llwyd members on a walk in Kate Roberts' footsteps, and went into the cemetery in Rhosgadfan to see her parents' grave. There were two boys, of ten and twelve, with us, and seeing them so small and young beside the grave sent shivers down our spines that afternoon.

Thomas and Gruffudd Parry have similar reminiscences of their childhoods on Gwyndy tyddyn on the outskirts of Carmel at the beginning of the twentieth century.

GWYNDY FIELD NAMES

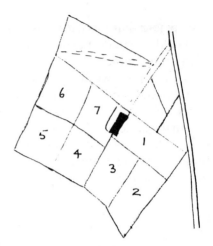

1. Cae cefn tŷ
2. Cae winllan eithin
3. Cae talcen gadlas
4. Cae bach
5. Cae pella
6. Cae isa
7. Cae o flaen drws

It was at Twll Coch Dorothea that I remember my father working most of the time. In summer he would start off at a quarter past six in the morning over the shoulder of Mynydd y Cilgwyn on stony paths down to Tal-y-sarn, to be at his 'bargain' *(bargen)* by seven o'clock, and he had a further ten minutes' walk from the quarry top down the ladders to his 'bargain'. He was a 'rockman' *(creigiwr)* and his task was to prise the rock off its bed in the most efficient way so that his partner in the shed could obtain a good number of slates off it.

Tŷ a Thyddyn, Thomas Parry

Opening and Closure Disagreements

As has already been stated, digging for slate on the common began with individuals and then partners extracting rock from near the surface. It's difficult to imagine how it was then, before the emergence of the enormous holes and waste heaps that surround us today.

In records for 1719 it is seen that inhabitants of Llandwrog parish are objecting to the work of some people from that parish, as well as from Llanwnda, Llanbeblig and Clynnog, in digging the earth on the common on Mynydd y Cilgwyn and by doing so digging on free pasture for Llandwrog parish residents. For people jealous of their rights the work of neighbours and strangers digging the mountain wasn't a matter they could ignore, and by 1719 there were so many diggers congregating and opening the mountain face with their work tools that the parishioners thought it was about time they put a stop to it.

There was quite a disturbance on the 1st of December, and the quarrymen turned their work tools into weapons. Consequently they were summonsed to appear before the Quarter Sessions in Caernarfon.

There was a 'tiles hole' on Mynydd y Cilgwyn according to the accusation, which brought harm and loss to Llandwrog parishioners, and impinged on their age-old rights.

Taking into account that at least seventy quarrymen were summonsed it is reasonable to assume that quite a bit of digging went on in Cilgwyn by 1719, and that the work was expanding daily. It wouldn't be unreasonable to assume that working had commenced on a smaller scale well before that year. There was an increase in trade after the country got rid of the Stewarts' oppression, which brought liveliness to several mines in the area, and it might be that this liveliness attracted the attention of some inhabitants to the riches in store in Cilgwyn. It is known that living conditions amongst the populace were quite severe at the beginning of the eighteenth century, and it was vital that many sought other means of sustenance. Putting all this together we believe that it would not be wrong to say that there was continual working in Cilgwyn Quarry from the early years of the eighteenth century, and because of this it can be considered to be the oldest quarry in the County. It must be remembered that the Quarter Session trouble did not halt mining in Cilgwyn.

Breision Hanes, W. Gilbet Williams

As the slate industry expanded, Lord Newborough of Glynllifon, the local landowner, took an interest in the ventures. Prominent landowners in other slate valleys also realised they could prosper and they sought to enclose the common land for their own gain; the Penrhyn and Vaenol estates were the most prominent by far. A petition by John Wynn of Glynllifon, dated May 1745, for mines and quarries in Caernarvonshire, shows that he secured mining rights for slate and ores on common land in eight parishes, including Llanwnda, for 31 years. During this period independent quarrymen were helping themselves to slate.

Within about five years (in 1767) food was dear and scarce in the country. At that time a ship laden with wheat arrived in Caernarfon, and the captain refused to share out the wheat, waiting for it to rise. All the Cilgwyn workers went down to Caernarfon to demand release of the wheat, and there was quite a commotion. It is said that one man was killed in the uproar. We make this comment to show that there were quite a number of men working in Cilgwyn at that time and the influence that they had on the country. Work was then going on in Cilgwyn in a number of scattered holes.

Chwareli Dyffryn Nantlle a Chymdogaeth Moeltryfan,
John Griffith, 1889

In 1774 a bid by his son, Thomas Wynn, to renew the lease was refused because his father had made no account of the profits. The Crown neglected its property during the early eighteenth century but matters changed when Robert Roberts was appointed overseer of mines and derelict land in 1791 He placed 'bargains' (part of the rock face to be worked) to numerous companies of quarrymen and he received rents from '40 persons for the liberty in part of a common called Kilgwyn', (Lindsay). Then Lord Newborough asserted his rights to Cilgwyn quarries and his agent ordered the quarrymen not to pay any more rent, and all but four agreed. The four who paid rent were set upon by a crowd of men who took possession of the quarry, in spite of Roberts' warnings. Roberts had no choice but to repay the quarrymen and in 1795 a court case discussed this. Even though Lord Newborough's lease had expired, his agent continued to pay and the Crown had to accept the old rent of 10 shillings per annum till 1790, when it was refused. When Newborough's lease renewal was refused there was no formal notice for him to yield his right to the quarries. An action of trespass was brought against Roberts in 1794 in relation to quarries on Cefn Du quarries above Waunfawr. The Crown's rights to the commons and mining rights were accepted by Newborough in 1773 but the Crown was mindful of the dangers of bringing actions to court because Roberts was striving to make the Crown's defence unpopular. According to Roberts:

> . . . the quarrymen naturally prefer holding under Lord Newborough, who has hitherto required from them an annual sum of only four pence per man which never amounted in total to more than 14s a year, a sum expended by Lord Newborough in an annual dinner for the Quarrymen.
>
> Lindsay

A benevolent Lord! The Crown agents were authorised to let the quarries for a sum not less than 5 shilling each.

The dispute was partly settled in 1800 when John Evans & Partners was given a lease for Cilgwyn quarry when the *Cilgwyn & Cefn Du Company* was formed. Cilgwyn covered 150 acres with enclosed land to the south and S.E. that included other quarries. Difficulties arose with some quarrymen who refused to acknowledge the lease, even though John Evans gave twelve of them a notice of trespass. Lord Newborough defended their case against the new company. A strange world! The company employed between 30 and 50

> . . . poor labourers residing in the neighbourhood who were not able to find any employment and consequent of the high price of corn were with their families reduced to great distress, slate being the only article for export from the county of Caernarvon.
>
> Lindsay

The work involved opening levels and clearing rubble left by previous quarrymen and consequently the company could only employ a few men. It was realised that it was impossible to defeat the independent quarrymen and their backer, Lord Newborough, and so work ceased.

'the quarrymen, supported by Lord Newborough, became riotous and declared that they would not quit and prevented the new lessees from working except in such parts of the quarry as they thought fit. There are 60 to 80 intruders upon Kilgwyn.

A History of the North Wales Slate Industry, Jean Lindsay

All these hindrances are reflected in the quarry accounts:

To workmen's wages and sundries	£627 11s 6d
To expenditure of the present quarter	£6 15s 2d
By slates made	£3 12s 6d

A warning was given in 1804 that a bid would be brought before the next parliamentary session to put forward a Measure to enclose the common land in Llanwnda, Llanllyfni and Llandwrog parishes. The commons were named thus: *'Clogwyn Melyn, Cilgwyn, Kim, Moeltryan, Rhos y Gadfa, Gallt y Coed Mawr* and *Braich Rhydd'* where most of the quarries were. The General Surveyor was opposed to enclosure; he suggested bringing a court action against the trespassers and his advice was heeded. Because of the threat of court action four men stated in 1895 that they would not in future 'disturb or molest the partners in the possession of the said Waste lands or in working any Quarries.' (Lindsay). It's difficult to make head or tail of such events! But here's one interesting story that proves poor 'tyddynwyr' could beat wealthy landowners, with a little bit of help:

The Penrhyn and Vaenol estates succeeded in taking possession of hundreds of acres of common land as a result of the Land Measure at the beginning of the nineteenth century. But Glynllifon estate failed even though it attempted to enclose all common land in Llandwrog and Llanllyfni parishes in 1826. The 'tyddynwyr' immediately contacted Grffith Davies . . . an eminent actuary in London with friends in high places in the city . . . a 'tyddynnwr's son from Mynydd y Cilgwyn, (Beudy isa above Groeslon) . . . and he put his friends to work to oppose the Bill in Parliament. Griffith Davies advised the 'tyddynwyr' to make an Appeal to Parliament to keep their homes.

They stated that most of them were quarrymen, that they had built homes on the common, some 40 years ago assuming it was free land . . . and that there were now 141 houses with nearly 700 living in them; that the mountain was rocky barren land, worth next to nothing until they, with hard labour after a days work, removed surface rocks, and tended and cultivated the soil . . . that they had heard there was a proposal to bring an Enclosure Measure before Parliament . . . And that they thought they had inadvertently transgressed the Crown's rights . . . and they asked to keep their homes and land, and to pay the Crown rent according to the land's value before they improved it.

The London Welsh held a meeting of support for the 'tyddynwyr', their speeches were printed in the *Times*. Griffith Davies arranged to publish their Appeal, and sent copies to MPs, and other VIPs, and secured members to introduce it in the House of Commons and the House of Lords. A fund was collected and three Welsh lawyers in London were to defend them.

In the end, when it became time for the Measure's second reading, Lord Newborough withdrew it, 'because there was a strong objection to it.'

To show their appreciation, the Mynydd y Cilgwyn 'tyddynwyr' brewed a cask of home beer and sent it as a gift to gladden the hearts of their benefactors in London.

Cau'r Tiroedd Comin, David Thomas

Similar difficulties persisted for years; e.g. a case of trespass as late as 1834. This was not surprising since Cefn Du and Cilgwyn commons contained numerous small quarries that had been worked for some time. Many of them were possessed by Cilgwyn Quarry and then re-let, Moeltryfan Quarry was contained in Cilgwyn's lease in 1825, which gave an additional piece of common to the company.

Dyffryn Nantlle contained numerous medium sized or small quarries, under various and changeable ownership, unlike Bethesda and Llanberis where two huge quarries were ruled with a rod of iron by Penrhyn and Vaenol estates. Even though worries arose during periods of uncertainty – when a quarry changed hands or when difficulties in clearing surface waste were experienced – because there were about three dozen quarries in the valley, a sacked worker could grab his tools and walk to a nearby quarry and seek work there.

I feel it an honour that I worked in Moeltryfan Quarry over summer holidays whilst in college during the early 1960s. I worked with about half a dozen others in a small shed at the far end of the quarry, what used to be Cors-y-Bryniau Quarry. One would cut the slate on the saw, while two old hands, my uncle Edwin Thomas and Robert Griffith from Cilgwyn, showed us youngsters how to split the rock, and they would then cut them to the right size on the 'trafael' (a long knife and bar). The blocks we had were fairly small, good enough for dampcourse, while the best ones would be sent to the big shed for the experienced quarrymen. I gained a particular satisfaction from being fairly successful with the craft of splitting even though my hands were covered in cuts and blisters and my arms and shoulders ached after loading the lorry with fresh roofing slate. I was very proud to tell my father about the work over 'swper chwarel' (quarry supper), especially as he had spent most of his working life in the quarries, but had to retire early after an accident while playing snooker of all things.

The Tyddynnod

Whilst discussing agricultural improvements during the eighteenth century A.H.Dodd states that one of the main hindrances was the existence of common land. The general belief was that communal ownership was no spur to land produce, while ownership of land turned sand into gold! Neither the landowners nor Crown agents had taken much interest in this stony and marshy ground up till then, but the trend for overstocking with sheep, and the likely increased profits from enclosed land, was a spur to them to follow the fashion and ask Parliament to enclose common land. But the Land Enclosure commissioners faced a problem in the existence of a large number of squatters who'd made their homes on the commons without legal rights, but often with the parish authorities' blessing.

Before the development of the quarries the commons reached much further down than they do today, but with the sudden increase in population as people came to work in the quarries, homes had to be found for them. There were no villages near the quarries, they were lower down, Llanwnda, Llandwrog and Llanllyfni around the parish churches, quite a distance for quarrymen to live and travel to work daily. The practical answer was to enclose a parcel of common land and erect a house on it, thus creating the smallholding, the tyddyn. The common shrivelled, the mountain wall moved higher up the slopes and the tyddynnod with their dry stone walled fields dotted the landscape. The map, 'Moeltryfan Enclosures', shows the 1790 mountain wall, halfway between Rhostryfan and Rhosgadfan now. The enclosure dates show the gradual movement up the pastureland, with the latest tyddynnod more or less on poorer land on Moeltryfan. The pattern of tracks and footpaths more or less corresponds to present roads and paths. It was around these that Rhosgadfan village was built later, between 1850 and 1900.

Several farms fringing on the common belonged to the Faenol, Llanfair and Plas Tirion estates and their owners and tenants in general resented seeing the spread of the tyddynnod, because it could result in the burden of increased rates if poor people lived on them. The tyddynwyr could turn their hand to varied tasks, stonewalling, hedgelaying, and carpentry, and there were craftsmen such as tailors, cobblers, weavers and smiths in the locality. The state of affairs in Llanwnda parish made it relatively easy to raise the tyddynnod; the landowners lived far enough from the common, and the earliest tyddynwyr were not strangers but the sons of neighbouring farms such as Wernlas Wen, Cae'r Odyn and Bodaden. They raised tyddynnod with their parents' consent, and amongst the earliest were those by Cae'r Odyn sons, namely Tan-y-gelynen, Tyddyn Canol and Pen-y-gwylwyr, today just above Rhostryfan. Several years later Glanrafon Hen, Gaerddu and Penffridd were enclosed, higher up on the lower outskirts of Rhosgadfan. Wernlas Wen's sons enclosed common on their boundary, Carreg Deimond, Tan-y-manod and Penceunant. Wernlas Ddu's sons enclosed lands as well, Thomas Williams at Ty'n Gadfan, Robert at Bryn Crin, John at Ty'n Rhosgadfan and daughter Catrin lived in Brynffynnon, all of them on the outskirts of Rhosgadfan by today.

Wrth ddod yn ôl yn llipryn	While coming back a hobbledehoy
O ladd y mawn a'r rhedyn,	From cutting peat and bracken
Caf de a sleisan o gig moch	I'll get a slice of bacon
Gan Martha Goch Cae'r Odyn.	From Martha Goch Cae'r Odyn.

William Bifan y Gadlys

The inhabitants of the farms nearest the common by now feared that the whole common could be enclosed. They had ancient rights on the common, where they came to raise peat. Life could be better in some respects for the tyddynwyr than for their neighbours on the farms because many of them were owners rather than tenants. Ownership made it possible to build more houses for the quarrymen because the tyddynwyr could sell a piece of land to erect a 'tŷ moel', a house with no land attached. The estates were unwilling to sell land for building houses, in fact they hardly sold any land until the end of the nineteenth century.

The parish's farmers raised peat from Gors Goch at the foot of Moeltryfan. Because of the spread of the tyddynnod the peat supply here was exhausted by about 1840 and it became necessary to go to another bog on the far side of Moeltryfan, Cors y Bryniau, which gave its name to the quarry and later to one of Kate Roberts' books. The railway came by the mid nineteenth century, which made coal available, and so coal was bought for a shilling a hundredweight by the gate rather than labouring to raise peat and carry it a long distance home.

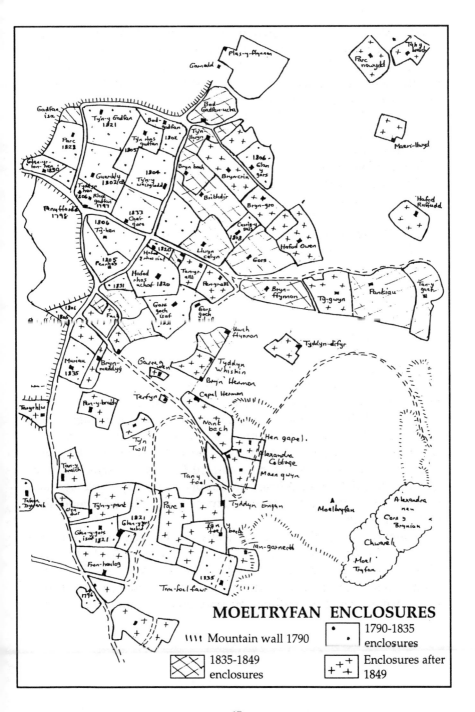

MOELTRYFAN ENCLOSURES

〰 Mountain wall 1790

1835-1849 enclosures

1790-1835 enclosures

Enclosures after 1849

The Moeltryfan tyddynnod were built from 1797 onwards and when the O.S. maps of 1889 were published the pattern of settlement was established. The rare maps from the first half of the nineteenth century show that many of the tyddynnod had been built by 1820, and all, more or less, by 1860. Amongst the earliest on Moeltryfan were:

Rhosgadfan 1797
Penffordd 1798
Tyddyn Hen 1800
Gaerddu Ddu 1802
Gaerddu Bach 1803
Ty'n Weirglodd 1804
Ty'n Rhosgadfan, Penffridd, Pantiau, Penrhos 1805
Tŷ Hen, Gorlan (Glangors today) 1806
Hafod-y-rhos Ucha ac Isa 1820
Parc 1828
Glanrafon Hen 1830
Cae'r Gors 1833
Brynffynnon 1836

After the decline of the slate industry, from the 1930s on some tyddynnod land was joined. Some houses were left empty as people moved into the villages, the men by now did not live near their workplace. It became more convenient to live in the village where there was a bus service to Caernarfon and other places where work was available. My parents, amongst other tyddynwyr from Cilgwyn, were forced to move to the new council houses in Carmel in 1938, Gwyrfai Rural District refused to supply electricity, sewerage and water to Cilgwyn and as a result many tyddynnod were condemned on health grounds.

Evidence of the old mountain walls can be seen in place names such as Llidiart Coch on the road between Rhostryfan and Rhosgadfan, and Llidiart y Mynydd, a house on the lower edge of Carmel where the road runs down towards Groeslon, which shows that Carmel was built entirely on previously common land before 1800.

Llidiart y Mynydd

Llidiard uwchlaw llidiardau – a godwyd
I gadw'r terfynau
Ar fynydd oer ei fannau,
A'i werth i gyd wrth ei gau.

John Thomas

A gate above gates was raised
To keep the boundaries
On the mountain of cold places,
Its whole purpose in its closing.

Thomas and Gruffudd Parry were brought up on two tyddynnod on the outskirts of Carmel, Gwyndy and Gwastadfaes. As in Kate Roberts' work, they give us detailed descriptions of life in the area when the quarry and tyddyn were essential elements of the way of life:

. . . Most of the area consists of tyddynnod enclosed from the mountain, as many of the names prove, Cae Ucha, Cae Forgan, Cae Ddafydd. It is likely there was an early enclosing and a later one, because the old mountain wall can be clearly recognised till today, namely the upper boundary of the line of farms, Cae Ucha, Cae Forgan, Caesion Mawr, Glynmeibon and Foty Wen, every one of them a farm of sufficient size to keep a family. On this line, a short distance below Carmel village, there was a gate across the road called Llidiart y Mynydd. Everybody of my age remembers it well. It was removed when the increase in traffic made it a nuisance.

Above the mountain wall and gate we have the small tyddynnod, between four and six acres, which represent the later enclosures . . . The tyddynnod came into being with the growth of the quarries. Before that the whole area was rather barren, empty mountain land.

Tŷ a Thyddyn, Thomas Parry

The farms could support a family during the first half of the twentieth century, as I remember well, but that is scarcely true by today, with all the subsidies. The milkman came around with a local

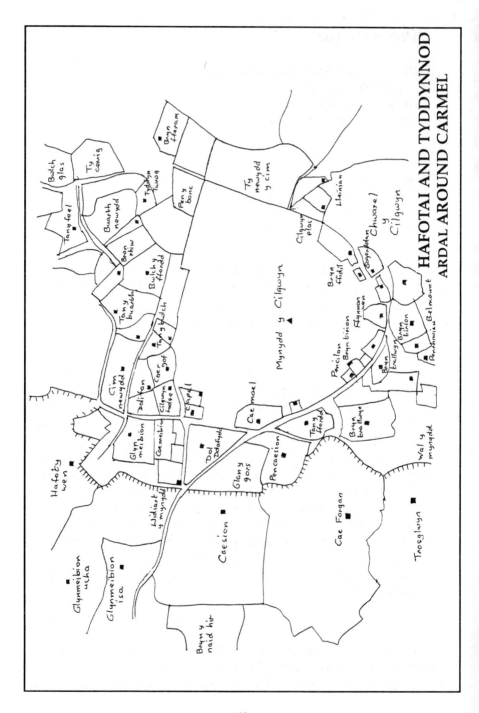

HAFOTAI AND TYDDYNNOD
ARDAL AROUND CARMEL

AGRICULTURAL DIVISIONS

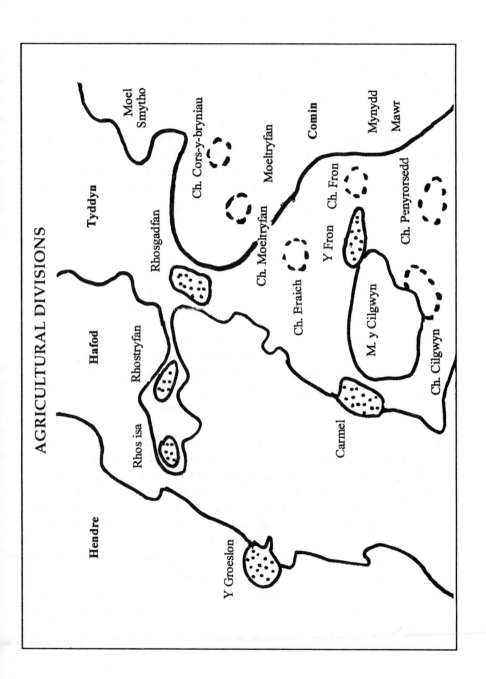

Hendre

Hafod

Tyddyn

Moel Smytho

Ch. Cors-y-bryniau

Comin

Mynydd Mawr

Moeltryfan

Ch. Moeltryfan

Rhosgadfan

Rhostryfan

Rhos isa

Ch. Braich

Y Fron

Ch. Fron

Ch. Penyrorsedd

M. y Cilgwyn

Ch. Cilgwyn

Carmel

Y Groeslon

herd's produce, local meat was available at the village butcher's and eggs and butter from the tyddynnod, and of course it all tasted so much better than what we get today.

One can clearly see the difference in area between the hafotai and tyddynnod on either side of the old mountain wall, very small fields on the tyddynnod, slightly bigger ones on the hafotai and even bigger still on the lower farms, the hendrefau. Thomas Parry refers to two enclosures. There were two periods and two kinds of enclosure. Between 1750 and 1800 enclosure by the hafotai's tenants, adding a bit of common to their lands e.g. Pencaesion to Caesion. In the second enclosure, between 1800 and 1850, farm sons and newcomers to the area were responsible for creating separate units, the tyddynnod. The area was previously called Bryn Melyn because of the proliferation of gorse on the slopes.

Between 1795 and 1895 about a million acres of common land was enclosed within Wales, comprising one-fifth of the country's area. As people from Môn and Llŷn came to work in the quarries, the easiest way for many to get a roof over their heads was to raise a 'Tŷ Unnos'. It was believed, without a legal basis, if you could raise a house, with a roof on it, between dawn and sunset, and get the chimney to smoke before sunrise, then whoever built it had a right to the Tŷ Unnos. The owners could take their time to complete the house afterwards. A powerful man was asked to throw an axe from the site to the four winds, and the land encompassed was enclosed, thus starting life on the tyddyn.

Local stone was used to build the house and field walls and there was plenty available on or near the surface, and of course slate was used for roofing. It's quite likely that stones from Iron Age sites were used during this building as well, as archaeologists have discovered extensive damage to some sites when excavating. They were small, single storey houses, with outhouses, cowshed, pigsty and hay barn, either attached or adjacent, and as often as not they were not very healthy homes. Remember that they were on mountain land, open to the elements, without tree shelter from wind and rain, and often built in haste. They had a small window to keep in the warmth, a kitchen and bedchamber, and 'croglofft' or 'taflod', a loft with stairs to climb to bed.

Ein tad yr hwn wyt yn y daflod	Our father up in the loft
Tyrd i lawr mae swper yn barod.	Come down supper is ready.

That's what would be whispered out of mum's hearing when going to bed long ago! Some later houses have bigger windows, and even one on each side of the door because they became easier to heat with the advent of coal. The field boundaries were drystone walls or stone and earth, with a few slate fences, but not as many as in other areas such as Mynydd Llandygái.

One thing worried her greatly, and that was the condition of the house. The kitchen where they lived was the only comfortable room. The bedchambers, especially the back one, were damp and wholly unhealthy for anybody to sleep in. Damp ran down the partitions, spoiling the wallpaper, and drops of water fell from the wooden ceiling on the bed during frosty weather. She would like to have an extension to the old house, so that she could have a best kitchen and two bedrooms at least. There were plenty of stones on Ffridd Felen to build such an addition, and clearing stones would benefit the land. But Ifan would have to blast them, which would entail even more work for him. Therefore, why did she dream?

Traed Mewn Cyffion, Kate Roberts

Improving the newly enclosed land meant hard labour, to turn it from rough mountain pasture to be permanent pasture, hay fields and even arable land for crops. It entailed laborious picking and digging till enough money was saved to buy a plough, endless clearing stones with more coming to the surface annually. Lime had to be spread regularly as the soil was very acidic, and then after several years manure would enrichen the soil, with the landscape's colour gradually being altered. By today the colour on many a tyddyn is merging back into mountain pasture, with exceptions like Hafod Ruffydd, where you can still see the contrast between the greenness of the fields and the purple and brown of the mountain.

Mi ddysgais wneud y gors	I learnt to make the marsh
Yn weirglodd ffrwythlon ir,	A fertile pasture,
I godi daear las	To raise green land
Ar wyneb anial dir.	Upon the face of wilderness.

'*Yr Arad Goch*', Ceiriog

The following statistics show how successful the tyddynwyr were in improving the soil.

LAND USE	1849					1991			
Tyddyn	**A**	**P**	**H**	**B**		**A**	**P**	**H**	**B**
Penceunant	17	17	48	17		0	95	0	5
Pantcelyn	0	65	36	0		0	65	35	0
Penisa'rhos	9	65	19	3		0	54	42	4
Pant Coch	24	12	45	18		0	62	0	33
Cae'r Gors	**33**	**11**	**55**	**1**		**0**	**28**	**0**	**72**
Penrallt						0	100	0	0

Cae'r Gors		**1849**	**Brynffynnon**
Field No.	**Land use**	**Field name**	
1506	A	Caeau ucha	1490 H
1507	P	" "	1491 P
1508	A	" "	John Hughes
			two & half acres
1508a	P	" "	
1509	H	Cae bach	
1510	H	Cae cefn tŷ	
1511	B		
1512	H	Cae dan tŷ	
1521	H	Y weirglodd	

6 acres   Anne Williams

A – arable   P – pasture   H – hay   B – buildings, waste
(Llanwnda Parish Tithe List 1849 and Survey by Gwydion Tomos, 1991)

A large percentage of arable land considering the tyddynnod's height, most likely root crops such as turnips and oats for animal feed, and vegetables for the family, potatoes, carrots, peas, broad beans and cabbage. The hay fields were essential for feed during the long, harsh

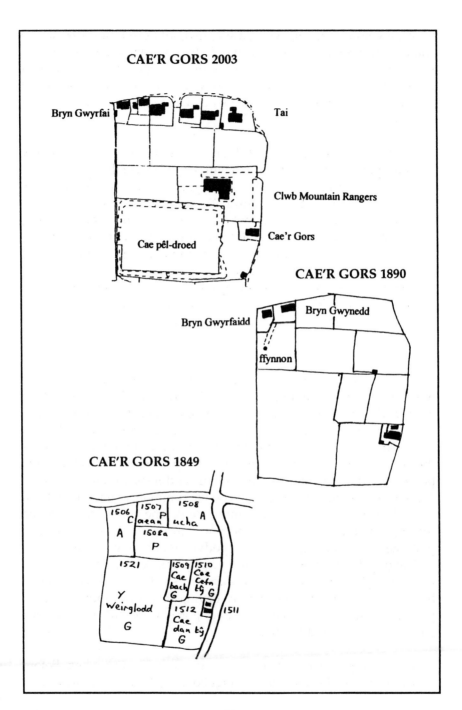

CAE'R GORS 2003

Bryn Gwyrfai

Tai

Clwb Mountain Rangers

Cae'r Gors

Cae pêl-droed

CAE'R GORS 1890

Bryn Gwyrfaidd

Bryn Gwynedd

ffynnon

CAE'R GORS 1849

1506 A

1507 C aean P

1508 ucha A

1508a P

1521

Y Weirglodd G

1509 Cae bach G

1510 Cae cefn tŷ G

1512 Cae dan tŷ G

1511

winters. Penrallt, the highest tyddyn, had not been built in 1849. The changes by 1991 are evident, with only two tyddynnod growing even hay, with no arable land at all. Letting the land for grazing is common today. The explanation for the 72% for Cae'r Gors is that houses and a Social Club have been built on the land, and a great deal of Cae Coch is garden by today.

> Mother and the boys and I are going to Bryn Ffynnon, my grandparents' house, for the haymaking. We climb and climb till we reach Pen'Rallt Fawr. We stop and look back. We can see more of Anglesey than from our house. We can see as far as Pont y Borth, and something else we cannot see from our house, the Lôn Wen, which goes over Moel Smatho to Waunfawr and to Heaven. It goes between the heather and reaches the mountain gate before falling to Alltgoed Mawr. We cannot see it after that. There are many people in the hay field and many children, my cousins and nieces, and we aren't allowed on top of the hayrick. We are nobody in this haymaking, and nobody takes any notice of us.

Y Lôn Wen, Kate Roberts

The tyddynnod had very little land, from two to six acres at most, often even less, with a number of small fields with dry stone walls or earth and stone banks, and sometimes gorse and thorn hedges. The tyddynwyr depended on the mountain pasture for their animals for a good part of the year, bringing the animals down onto the fields over the bleak winter months. Cattle and sheep were mostly kept, some ponies, and there would usually be pigs and hens around the house. The tyddynwyr had grazing rights on the common, a practice that still exists but is not used to the same extent. The common would be managed by the tyddynwyr or 'porwyr', graziers as they were called, with the rights being given to the tyddyn and not to individuals.

Digging for peat was a common practice, with numerous bogs, Cors Goch, Cors Tan Foel, Cors Dafarn, Cors y Bryniau and a long one by Llyn Ffynhonnau, every family having their own spot to dig for peat in early summer. Heather and gorse were cut as bases for hayricks and for lighting fires.

> Within about three stone throws from our house was a bog. Before winter came the men from neighbouring tyddynnod would be

busy cutting peat in long pieces the size of building bricks and then leaving them to dry. I only once saw a spade specially made for cutting peat with a blade on one side. With that spade every piece of peat would be exactly the same size and shape but not so with an ordinary spade. My father would carry them and lay them in a heap in the windowless aisle at the back of the house. The peat fire had no flame but one or two lumps of coal would be a help to produce a flame to cheer the hearth.

Dwy Aelwyd, Lisi Jones

The bog by Llyn Ffynhonnau is probably referred to here.

Another place we went to was Mynydd Grug or Moel Smythaw . . . We would go there to pull heather for the rick's base before the hay harvest . . . The hay would be placed on this base, and by winter, when the rick would be cut for feeding the cows, it would have withered. One of our tasks as children before going to school would be to carry some of the heather to the house in a box for lighting the fire the next day.

Atgofion, Kate Roberts

The heather would be set alight over part of the common to improve the pasture, ditches were opened, the sheep kept within their 'cynefin', heft, and later fences and gates were erected to stop the cattle and sheep from wandering down into the villages. Talking of cynefin, because they raised their own stock the lambs would naturally learn from the ewes, which is not always the case today, when sheep are brought in from afar to graze on the common, and consequently they will be more inclined to roam, as they don't know where they belong.

The tyddyn was never a viable agricultural unit to support a family, but the produce from land and animals – vegetables, milk, butter, wool, eggs and occasionally meat – were welcome supplements to the quarryman's wage and secured healthy food for the family, and so raised their standard of living in an age when large families were the norm.

Too much emphasis is often placed on the quarryman's poverty. They probably lived from hand to mouth, with no savings, depending on the whims of the 'bargain' for wages and the weather for produce, but they did not starve. It was certainly a hard life, within the confines of quarry and tyddyn, but most succeeded in keeping from debt, and a few to better their state a little.

This was our home for twenty-six years, at the end of the last century and the beginning of this one. (19th & 20th) It was in Cae'r Gors' kitchen that we learnt our verses for Sunday School and Fellowship meeting, made our school tasks, read stories and newspapers, played ludo and dominoes in the evening, listened to father singing 'Gelert Ci Llywelyn' on Saturday night, listened to mother reciting pieces of Eben Fardd and breaking into song every now and again. It was here that we ate the plain good food we had, everybody with his place by the big long table. Because we had two cows in the shed, two pigs in the sty and hens on the fields, we were not short of butter, eggs and milk.

Our big meal was 'swper chwarel', quarry supper, the meal we had after father and my brothers came home from the quarry. We had 'lobscows' or liver and swede mash or bacon and pea mash. We had plenty of swedes in the shed, to cut up for the cows. We only had pudding on baking day and Sunday when the oven was on the go.

Then about nine we had a cup of tea and a cheese sandwich, or haddock … we had oatcakes with the haddock, oatcakes that Elin Jones Penffordd had made, big ones curling like a basket.

Because our tyddyn was small, the fields were small except one, the wet meadow, difficult to dry its hay. Cae dan Tŷ, Cae Cefn Tŷ, Cae Bach, Y Caeau Ucha. I liked strolling through the fields on my own. Cae Bach was a likeable one; there was a large flat boulder at its bottom, and on this I would make my 'little house', and collect things to make a dresser by putting a slate on two stones. I spent a lot of time sitting on this boulder, and in September there would be plenty of blackberries in Cae Bach. Oats would be grown on half of it some seasons and potatoes another time. The corn would be threshed with a flail in the corner on clean sacks. I remember that once my cousin R.Alun Roberts and his brother Hughie came one pleasant Saturday afternoon, and we all took turns to flail and had good fun. The straw would be used under the pigs and the oats as chickenfeed. The fields had earth banks with pretty heather and gorse growing on them, and bilberries, and it was pure pleasure picking bilberries off them at harvest time, threading them on a hair like beads and then pulling them into our mouths.

Atgofion, Kate Roberts

The houses were very small, with hardly room to move considering the heavy furniture and size of the families. We have our kitchen, dining room and lounge or two these days, and every labour saving device. The tyddynnod made do with one living room, one bedroom next door and a loft up the ladder above, but they had a welcoming hearth. This is what Cae'r Gors was like inside:

While standing in the middle of the kitchen floor my whole childhood appeared before me. That day in the kitchen I saw it exactly as it was seventy years ago. The red and blue tiles that I would wash when home on holiday and on Saturday morning. It looked big then when I took the table and chairs out, and washed under the sofa.

It was here in the kitchen that most of the housework was done. Baking, washing, ironing, as well as cleaning the kitchen itself. On the fire under the large chimney bacon and other things would be fried, we would boil the potatoes and vegetables on the fire. We would bake bread in the oven. There were two ovens under the chimney, a large one, with space for a fire underneath, and a small one besides the fire.

A chain hung above the grate, but we didn't use it. White clothes would be boiled on the fire in an oval saucepan with a handle on washing day.

On one kitchen wall there was a two-door plain mahogany glass cupboard, a beautiful, broad and tall mahogany clock, another three door glass cupboard; this was of white oak with three mahogany panels on the lower part of it, with the veined mahogany pattern distinct on hem. Crockery was kept in the cupboards' lower halves and clothes, such as bedclothes, in the bottom of one, and suits and hats in the other.

On the other side, under the window, there was a large strong sofa with horsehair backs and sides to it. Mother had asked a carpenter to make a solid wooden seat for it and she had covered it with oilcloth. When visitors were expected cushions with a cover of colourful material were placed on the sofa. By the sofa there was a tall cupboard whose back formed a sort of porch where clothes were hung when entering the kitchen. Even though every task was done in the kitchen, it would be clean as a lamp by afternoon, and we would have our tea after coming home from school and 'swper chwarel' in it, in a comfortable place.

Behind the kitchen was the dairy, a roomy enough one, a row of pots for keeping milk on one side with round slates on top of them, and one different milk pot with a wooden cover, where we kept the bread, our own bread. There was a table there as well; on this the butter would be treated on churning day – and the pastry for tarts, a large table with drawers as well, called a 'cupboard table' by some, and enough shelves to keep crockery, and the churn as well. There was a grate in the dairy, but it was only used occasionally when the wind would be from an advantageous direction. There was a large wooden mangle as well, and above it in the roof was a window that lit up the whole place.

There were two bedchambers, the back one by the dairy, with only a wooden bed painted white, a small table and chair in it. It was an old wainscot bed with the top sawn off. I loved sleeping in this bed because the window opened on to the hay barn, and the smell of grass came in, and I could hear the clucking of the hens.

The front bedchamber was bigger than the back one, with room for a large bed in it, chairs, a washing table with jug and basin, a dressing table that we called 'glass table', a big oak chest of drawers made by a local carpenter. An old fashioned clock on the partition, and from this one my brother taught me to tell the time. There was a fireplace in it that pulled well when needed during sickness. Because it was the best chamber it had an oilcloth and rug on the floor. This is where we would be when ill, and I have happy memories of having meals in bed in this chamber when I was on the mend.

We had a loft as well, with two beds in it, small beds right by the roof, and without room for anything else but a small table. My chore on Saturday morning would be to scour the ladder used to go up to it.

Atgofion, Kate Roberts

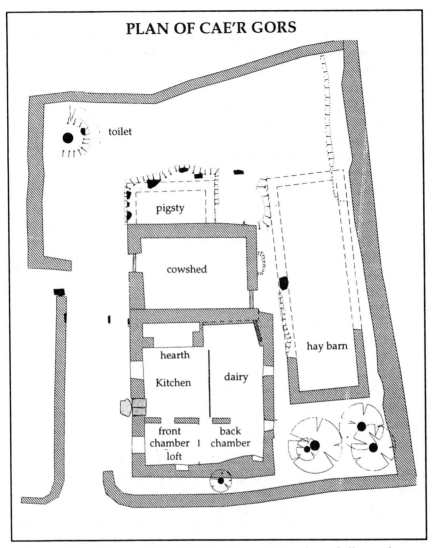

PLAN OF CAE'R GORS

toilet

pigsty

cowshed

hay barn

hearth

Kitchen   dairy

front   back
chamber   chamber
loft

After reading this typically detailed description, hopefully we have a clear picture of the interior of the house before our eyes. Where did thriftiness disappear to I wonder?

These are the people involved with Cae'r Gors from the beginning, since it was built in 1827 or 1833.

1827/33 – Robert Pritchard and his family were the first occupiers most likely.
1841 – Census – Robert Pritchard.

Early 1840s – A Sunday School was held here. Rhosgadfan chapel was built in 1861.

1850 – Tithe – occupier was Anne Williams

1851 – Census – Owen Jones, Bodgadfan, born Llanwnda parish, and his wife Anne, daughter of Wernlas Ddu, Rhostryfan.

1861 – Anne Williams, head of family.

1883 – death of Owen Jones.

John Jones, his son, and his wife Mary Thomas/Jones, Penrhos.

1892 – death of John Jones.

Mary moved to Bod Elen, a house built for her in Rhosgadfan, Glanfa today.

1895 – Owen and Catherine Roberts, Kate Roberts' parents moved from Bryn Gwyrfai, renting from Mary Jones.

Owen worked in Cilgwyn quarry between 1861 and 1907, then a spell in Liverpool and at Cors y Bryniau till 1927 when he was 79 years old.

1901 – Census – Owen 50, Catherine 46, half brother John 17, Kate 10, Richard 8, Evan 5, David 2, half sister Jane a frequent visitor.

1921/23 – Owen and Catherine moved to Maesteg, a house in Rhosgadfan.

1921/23 – John and Jane Jones.

1926/28 – John and Jane moved to Ty'n Llwyn.

John William Hughes, Bryn Awelon, entrepreneur, coal merchant, quarryman in Fron and Hen Fraich, the first bus service from Rhosgadfan to Caernarfon.

1931 – Death of Owen Roberts, Maesteg.

1932 – JWH sold Cae'r Gors to his father, William Richard Hughes.

1959 – sold to Thomas Gwilym Hughes and Elen, son of JHW's brother.

They were the last occupiers.

1961 – TGH sold to Brian and Rosina Jones, but they did not live there.

1964 – Kate Roberts decided to buy Cae'r Gors and present it to the nation in her memory and her work.

1965 – BJ sold the house, but not the land, to the care of trustees (Islwyn Ffowc Ellis, John Gwilym Jones, R. E. Jones, Elwyn Roberts, Cassie Davies, J. R. Cadwaladr, Ifor Wyn Williams and J. E. Jones) to keep as a controlled ruin.

1971 – Kate Roberts presented the house to the nation.

1995 – it was decided to raise money to renew Cae'r Gors, Cyfeillion Cae'r Gors came into being, Guto Roberts one of the chief instigators.

1997 – two remaining trustees, Islwyn Ffowc Ellis and Ifor Wyn Williams, handed over Cae'r Gors to Cyfeillion Cae'r Gors.
Guto and Marian Roberts, Norman Williams and Eirug Wyn mainly responsible for launching a fundraising campaign to renovate the house.
2005 – Canolfan Dreftadaeth Cae'r Gors established.

Richard Cadwaladr (1819-1893), Kate Robert's grandfather on her maternal side, was originally from Llanaelhaearn. He worked in Dinorwig Quarry, married Catrin Robinson (1827-1912) from Groeslon and went to live in Pantcelyn, Caeau Cochion on the outskirts of Rhostryfan. They had thirteen children, twelve of whom lived to marriageable ages.

The paternal side of her family came from Llŷn. Her grand grandparents came from Garn Fadryn to Llanllyfni and then to Hafod y Rhos on Moeltryfan.

Brynffynnon was built in 1836, with John Hughes (d.1847) from Wernlas Ddu and his wife Catherine (d.1871) living there. Owen and Catherine Roberts, Kate Roberts' grandparents, moved there in 1851, with Owen, her father, seven months old and his brother, Robert, two. Around 1901 the couple moved to Hafod y Rhos Isa and Owen Roberts died in 1904 aged 77. The family connection with Brynffynnon persisted as they exchanged houses with Kate, their daughter, and her husband, and their son Morris lived there later. The graves of the two generations, parents and grandparents, are in Rhosgadfan cemetery. The family history is typical of the early quarrymen's background: moving to the area from neighbouring parishes, then from Môn and Llŷn, with some movement to and fro, from tyddyn to tyddyn or to a 'tŷ moel' in old age, all of it local movement.

It is worth quoting fully from Thomas Parry's *Tŷ a Thyddyn* as it gives us a lively and detailed picture of life on a tyddyn. The booklet is one of the series of Penygroes Library annual lectures, and since the publication of the first in 1967 by Gwilym R. Jones, we have had such a wealth of material on various aspects of life in Dyffryn Nantlle. It's a priceless series for anybody with an interest in local history.

The tyddyn was about four or five acres, at most, won from the mountain, and the soil was not much more than a spade's depth, but wonderfully fertile because of the periodical ploughing and regular manuring. The main crop was hay, and plenty of potatoes were grown for the year and swedes, carrots, broad beans and peas. Occasionally a small plot of oats would be sown, and after being harvested, threshed with a flail . . . the grain was taken to Llwyn Gwalch Mill so as to get material for porridge and oatcakes . . .

One of the problems on a tyddyn like Gwyndy where we lived was pasture during spring. There were seven fields – cae cefn tŷ, cae winllan eithin, cae talcen gadlas, cae bach, cae pella, cae isa and cae o flaen drws. Cae o flaen drws (field in front of the door) was the only one grazed, but somewhere needed to be found for the two cows while the early pasture greened, and that was the mountain. The mountain grass was very short, but the cows prospered on it for some weeks every spring. We had another source as well. A sister of my grandmother, Anti Margiad, lived with her son, John Roberts, in Pen-ffynnon-wen in Cilgwyn, and she had two strips of fields, and we walked the cows there in the morning and went for them in the afternoon, about a mile away. It was very easy to walk animals on the roads then because there was hardly any traffic worth mentioning. When the cattle grazed the mountain, they came home of themselves without any bother, and about four o'clock every tyddyn's cow could be seen standing patiently by its own gate. One of the most important tasks on the tyddyn was to gather the hay sometime at the beginning or middle of July. The order I remember first was to cut the hay with a scythe, and several days before time they had to be honed on the stone. And this was one example of co-operation. My father had a good reputation for honing scythes, and some of our neighbours would bring their scythes to Gwyndy for my father to treat them . . .

They came later to cut the hay, and what a wonderful sight was four or five strong men swinging the scythes through the hay with easy regular movements, their footprints two parallel rows between the swathes . . . If the weather was fine, the hay would be ready to be carried to the enclosure and made into a hayrick within a few days. The hayrick's base would be prepared with small mountain gorse or bracken . . . On carrying day a good number of neighbours would come to help; and really without them the hay could not be brought to shelter. The day's work was one of the most orderly and systematic, and consequently exceptionally effective.

About half a dozen women would begin to rake along one side

of the field till they had a fairly substantial rank. Then there came a man with a hayfork, and his task was to place some hay on a double rope running through a wooden link. Following him another man tied the load and lifted it onto the carrier's back, who'd tied an apron on his head, the string around his waist, in case the seed went between his shirt and skin. With this method a crew of twelve, including four carriers, could clear a field in no time at all, quicker in fact than a horse and cart.

Tŷ a Thyddyn, Thomas Parry

Dringo i'r bonc; datod y clymau tyn
A roed pan blygwyd y mynyddoedd hyn,
Rhoi rhaw yn naear ddicra'r Cilgwyn noeth,
A phladur yn ei fyrwellt hafddydd poeth –
Troi dy dawedog nerth, aberth dy fraich,
Yn hamdden dysg i ni, heb gyfri'r baich.

'Fy Nhad', Tomas Parry

Climb to the gallery; free the tight knots
Made when these mountains buckled,
Place a spade in Cilgwyn's bare earth,
And a scythe in its short grass on a hot summer's day –
Turning your quiet srength, your arm's sacrifice,
To learning's leisure for us, without counting the cost.

His brother, Gruffudd, describes letting the cows loose to graze on the common:

The mountain is not much different summer or winter – the seasonless greatness. Yet, it has changed colour slightly by early summer like this and the short grass amongst the heather clumps has greened. The two have their path on the verge beside the road where wayfarers, man and animal, have eroded the earth red trying to evade the metalling and stones. It merely needs opening the mountain gate for them and they will find their way to Pant yr Eira level or higher and nobody will see them till it's time for the men to come from the quarry.

Blwyddyn Bentra, Gruffudd Parry

63

Pen-ffynnon-wen's son, John Roberts, married my grandmother, her second husband and not my blood grandfather, but he was the only one I remembered. My brothers were born in one of the other houses in Pen-ffynnon-wen and lived there till they were six and nine, neighbours to Taid and Nain and their younger children. By the time I came on the scene the two families lived next door but one again in the new council houses in Carmel, forced from their tyddynnod in Cilgwyn by Gwyrfai Rural Council. That was the beginning of the end for the tyddynnod.

I remember that exact method of haymaking mentioned when I would go with my father to nearby tyddynnod, Ty'n Gadlas, Caesion Isa, Bryn Derwen, and especially Maes Gwyn opposite our home. Hayforks and rakes in a line by the gate waiting for ready hands. The children would usually rake with the women. I can also remember shorter ropes and therefore lighter loads on them, and we lads looked forward eagerly to the day we'd be considered big and strong enough to carry a load, but unfortunately I was rather a lightweight. My father and others were prepared to lose half a day's wages to repay a favour, especially when the weather threatened to take a turn for the worse and there was a rush to get the hay under cover.

My father didn't keep animals except hens, but Bryn Glas' cow would graze one of the fields, and Bryn Glas would also get the hay from the other field as well, in exchange for milk and butter. Father used to cut the grass in the back garden with the scythe he'd brought with him from Pen-ffynnon-wen and I would observe him at it, the grass falling so effortlessly. When I became old enough to give it a try I soon realised that brute force wasn't enough.

'Don't fight with it, let the blade run smoothly, you need a proper swing,' would be father's advice. The old scythe is in the shed but I dare not use it, as the handle is full of woodworm holes. But I can still look at it . . .

Uwchgwyrfai Common

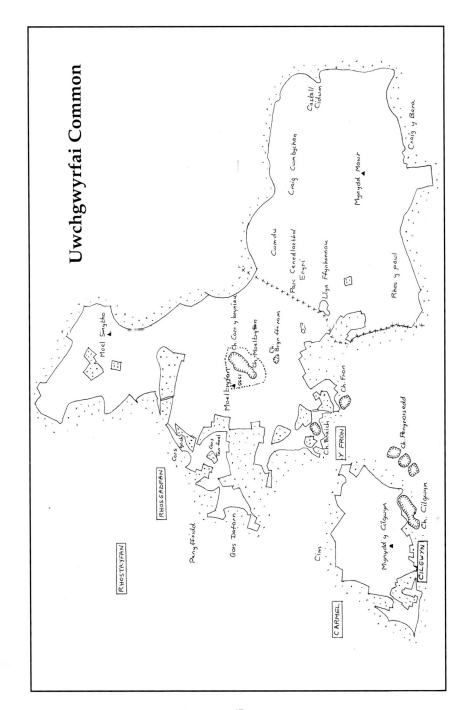

Cae'r Gors, Kate Roberts' home

Ty'n Llwyn, Rhosgadfan

Bryn Ffynnon, Rhosgadfan, where Kate Roberts' grandparents lived

Bryn Hafod, Lisi Jones' childhood home

Splitting and dressing

Hermon Chapel, Moeltryfan

Cilgwyn Chapel

Cors y Bryniau Quarry

Coed-y-brain settlement

70

Gwerin y Graith site, Parc Glynllifon: excerpt from Y Lôn Wen, *Kate Roberts*

YR HÊN CHWARELWR CYMREIG

WYN WILLIAMS

The Old Quarryman

Y Gwyndy, Carmel – Thomas and Gruffudd Parry's family home.

Cilgwyn and Penyrorsedd quarries and Dyffryn Nantlle

Mynydd y Cilgwyn and Cilgwyn Quarry

Yr Eifl from Foel Smytho

Moeltryfan and Fron Village

Cors y Bryniau and Moeltryfan

Blaenfferam, Y Fron

Moeltryfan from the Fron side

Penffynnon-wen, Cilgwyn
(photo: Ieuan Thomas)

Tŷ Newydd, Y Bryn

Tal-y-braich, Moel Smytho

Dressing on the 'trafael'

Splitting

CILGWYN TYDDYNNOD

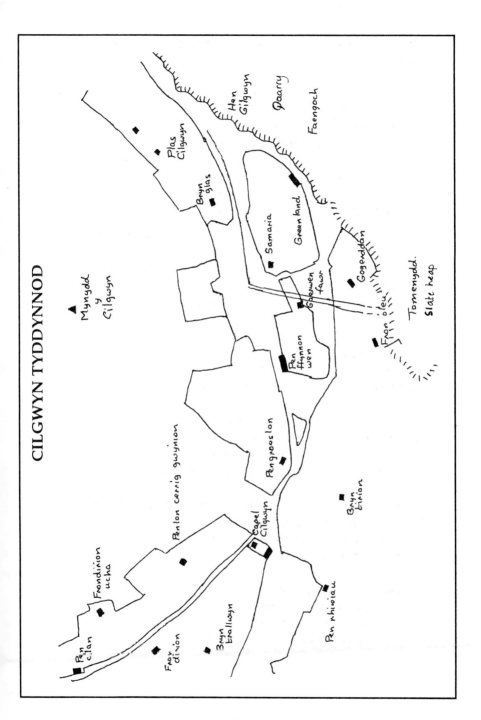

This is a verse from a poem by my uncle, brought up in Pen-ffynnon-wen:

> Old Cilgwyn, the romance of long gone times
> Hovers around your peaks in hordes;
> And yesterday's voices still on the wind,
> An everlasting echo of the old times,
> And you, if you would like before your time comes
> To feel your heart young and free,
> Listen to the bard's advice, 'Go forth and stand
> On Cilgwyn's summit on a summer's day.

> *'Cilgwyn 1934'* Griffith John Roberts

My uncle was twenty-four when he wrote that poem, and here's another one in reply to my book of walks, *'Llwybrau Lleu,* nearly half a century later, but the attraction and longing, 'hiraeth', remains:

> I followed Lleu's paths from an easy chair
> Without sweaty brow or wet feet,
> Without the aid of stick or burden of laden sack,
> And this was well considering my age.

> I returned again on remembrance's wing
> To the familiar acres that I knew,
> And a trek to Foel or Llyn Ffynhonnau
> Was only a step or two without losing wind.

> To experience again the romance of my childhood haunts,
> Taste the secret of bygone days,
> The treeless world and blue slate tips,
> It was our heaven, we knew of no other.

> The old, old names, so magical by now,
> As in the golden times gone by,
> Penffynnon Wen, Samaria, Cae Aeronwy,
> Llwyn Gwalch, Bryn Neidr and Pant Du.

I'm not likely to travel them again
Nor follow Lleu's paths ever more,
But thanks for safeguarding them,
I shut my eyes, and walk along them.

Griff, 1981

Without today's machines haymaking involved much labour with rakes and forks, with the changeable weather needing great haste when the hay dried well:

It's a hot morning in July, haymaking day. Father and his friends from the quarry will come home about midday, and some neighbours have already arrived and begun to turn over the hay. I can hear the sound of hayrakes keeping time with each other and the hay sounding like silk paper. Before going out to the field I enter the dairy once again to have a peek at the delicacies. There is a long row of glass bowls on the table full of rice pudding with plenty of eggs in it, the pudding skin yellow and smooth like the breast of the canary in the cage by the table. Its smell and look makes my mouth water. I wonder if there'll be enough for everybody. We're not to ask for more in front of strangers. After going to the field I have a go with the rake, but it's too big, and my turn is untidy. The women's arms are all the same and move together, and they go down and down to the bottom of the field before turning and come up and up again, the same kind and same time and same dud-dud sound all the time.

Y Lôn Wen, Kate Roberts

Another detailed account typical of Kate Roberts. Can you hear the rakes and smell the rice pudding I wonder?

The writer and poet Lisi Jones spent her life in Y Fron, my parents referred to her as Lisi Jones Garreg Fawr.

My grandfather was from Caergybi . . . He came to Fron to work as a labourer in the quarries as he had no quarrying background. My reason for mentioning that he was a labourer is that I feel it a privilege to pay homage to my grandmother as a mother and housewife . . . She never failed to manage to keep out of debt.

Rather she had a bit left over. I remember mother saying how as a child she would take a loaf to a little lonely neighbour who lived on her own on a nearby hillock because she had to depend on neighbours' kindnesses.

To raise her children, my grandmother used to deal in bulk buying. A sack of flour, bags of oat flour and sugar, a cheese and side of bacon. She made brawn from a sheep or pig's head and today's brawn makers would be glad of her recipe . . .

We went to live in Bryn Hafod, tucked by Mynyddfawr's foot . . . We weren't in Bryn Hafod for long but the experience of living in the environment left a lasting impression on a curious child. There was an ash tree in front of the cottage and when spring came we used to hang on its branch our pair of doves' cage and once a cuckoo came onto the branch and the three birds burst into song together. It was a pleasant unique occurrence and its notes still echo on my hearing.

Many a time I also went with the old man Daniel Roberts, Penrhyn, to send the old black cow to graze on Bryn Castell's field, a tyddyn on Mynyddfawr's slope. The house had long been a ruin then and the rushes and rough grass has long ago taken over from the pasture. It was pleasant to go on carefree days to pick bilberries, crowberry too, and cranberry and have a cake or tart, while they were in season.

Dwy Aelwyd, Lisi Jones

Only a yard or two remains of Penrhyn's walls, sufficient to shelter a sheep or walker on the open path. Bryn Hafod's ruins is amongst a cluster of tyddynnod between Llyn Ffynhonnau, Y Fron and Nantle, an enchanted place facing the sun and Nantlle ridge, and the remains of a square enclosure can be seen above Llyn Ffynhonnau where once stood Bryn Castell, on its own on the mountainside. This was a ruin even a century ago.

Hen Dŷ (Old House)

Muriau chwâl ac anialwch – wedi mynd
  Y mae pob rhyw degwch
  Y tân hwyr a'r tynerwch
  A'r llaw a fu'n sgubo'r llwch.

Alun Jones

Scattered walls and wilderness – gone
  Is all kind of beauty –
  The late fire and tenderness
  And the hand that swept.

It was a confined world, between tyddyn and quarry, work and rest and striving to live, with the women's living conditions even more confined, tied to life's tethers.

'Hullo,' over the house. Dafydd Gruffydd was waking at six o'clock on he morning of his seventieth birthday to go to his work in the quarry . . .

Beti Gruffydd had always been a homely one. There was not much room in her life for anything except work and treating the milk and butter. Her interest was at home. When she took an interest in anything outside her home, it came by book or newspaper . . . She had never been to the quarry. She had not the slightest idea in what kind of place her husband worked in. The nearest connection between her and the quarry were her husband's food tin, his fustian clothes and his slate dust covered wages . . .

There was five pounds of butter on the round slate, the churn was drying out in the sun, and the house was cleaned by the time Dafydd Gruffydd came home at midday. After his dinner of new potatoes and buttermilk, he went out to pare the thorns in the fields. That's how he did every Saturday, and in the evening he would go out to do something around the farm. He was never seen idle. On one appearance his life circle was as confined as his wife's. Mixing with the quarrymen was the only thing that broadened it.

She looked at him again swinging the sickle like the wind with a

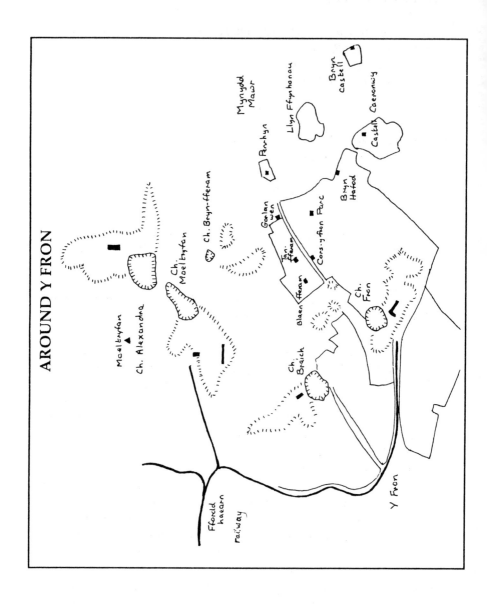

AROUND Y FRON

Maeltyfan
Ch. Alexandra

Ch. Moeltyfan

Ch. Bryn-ffenan

Parchyn

Mynydd Mawr

Llyn Ffynhonau

Bryn Castell

Castell Caenonwy

Gorlan wen

Corsyfron Parc

Bryn Hafod

Tan y Fron

Blaen Fron

Ch. Fron

Ch. Braich

Y Fron

Ffordd haearn
railway

complaint coming from his breast like an echo stone with every stroke.

And she thought, 'He'll be lying in that cemetery in a while, with his hands crossed forever.'

Rhigolau Bywyd, Kate Roberts

Even though life on a 'tyddyn' could be very hard, there was this strange attachment to the unique way of life, this duality between industry and agriculture and the satisfaction gained from tending the land and rearing stock, as is evident in this quotation:

It was one of those summer mornings, when gossamer threads are thick, or rather thin on the hedges, and the sound of quarrymen's feet and talk is heard like bees in the near distance. William Gruffydd stood leaning against the small garden gate looking far away without looking anywhere in particular. There was a longing look in his eyes; but, in any case, that's how he always looked . . . That morning he looked more nostalgic than usual, and too meditative to take any notice of the quarrymen who waved to him on passing.

Three years had gone by since he gave up the quarry and moved from Bryn y Fawnog to Bodlondeb, from tyddyn to house. A short time before that his son Guto had gone to America, and it was he who had persuaded his parents to move to the house and leave the quarry for a bit of rest at the end of their days. But Margiad died within two years of moving; and her last words were about cattle and pigs and such animals . . .

After Margiad's death he had a young girl to keep house, but neither she nor the house hardly saw him from morning till night, he spent his time leaning on the garden gate or talking to the road workers. In a word, he was lost from the day he left the quarry. It's true he had fond memories of Bryn y Fawnog.

'Newid Byd', *O Gors y Bryniau*, Kate Roberts

It is interesting to note her suggestive choice of names for the two homes – Bryn y Fawnog suggesting hardship, and Bodlondeb an easy life, but that is not the way that William Gruffydd saw things.

That is how the unique landscape was shaped on the weather-beaten slopes; the pattern of tyddynnod and their minute fields within a stone's throw of the quarries, and the quarryman-tyddynnwr and his family tending the meagre land, and all of it depending on the slate industry's success. This way of life has gone but the mute testimony remains. This locality, along with the rest of Dyffryn Nantlle, has been registered as a Landscape of Exceptional Historical Interest by CADW, who've also denoted a number of tyddynnod as Listed Buildings, so that the hive of activity that was can be kept for the ages to come.

CADW Listed Buildings in the common's vicinity:

Parish   Betws Garmon – Tal-y-braich
Llanwnda – Ty'n Llwyn, Glangors, Cae'r Gors, Rhosgadfan, Tyddyn Difyr, Ty'n Twll, Pen-y-bwlch, Gorphwysfa, Tegfan.
Llandwrog – Tyddyn Engan, Bwthyn Buarth Newydd, Buarth Fawr, Caeronwy Isaf, Pen-bwlch Bach, Bwlch-y-ffordd, Tŷ Newydd.
Llanllyfni – Parc.

Llainfadyn tyddyn's house was moved to Sain Ffagan in 1956, and in 2002 Cae Adda cowshed, Waunfawr, was moved and placed alongside Llainfadyn. This is a description of Llainfadyn:

The wall's huge boulders came from nearby fields, with many of them reaching through the whole wall, their heads jutting out on the outside. It's easy to see from outside which is the living room, with one chimney and window. There was no need for a fire on the other side, nor as much light. Between the door and the living room there is a huge slate to keep the wind from the fire. The building date, 1762, is carved on the mantelpiece. Under the fire there is an iron with small holes in it and a hole underneath, the 'uffern', (hell). Instead of taking the ash and cinders out daily it was swept into the 'uffern' and then emptied at the weekend. This warm spot was ideal for placing weak chicks to strengthen, and that is one explanation for the saying, 'Cyw a fegir yn uffern, yn uffern y mynn fod.' (A chick reared in hell seeks to remain in hell). The house's floor is of hardened earth. To keep the damp from rising to the furniture they were placed on a low slate platform. Another remarkable item is the bread car hanging from the roof, to keep food from mice's teeth. The other half of the house is filled with two box beds. This type of house was described thus in 1811: ' Their houses are well furnished, with shining clock, chest of drawers, brass cupboards for clothes, crockery and pewter all in their place; and the weather is kept out of their beds by boarding them above and on three sides, so that they look like a kind of box'.

Planks were placed above the box beds to form an open loft. A ladder was necessary to climb into it. Because of this, this kind of building was called 'bwthyn croglofft' (loft cottage) or 'tŷ taflod'. The parents and elder children slept in the beds and the younger children in the loft. In later examples of this kind of house a proper loft was built in this part of the house, with its front closed. The loft cottage is a common form of house on the western shores of Wales from Môn to Penfro, built between 1770 and 1870. Llainfadyn is really the earliest dated example.

Welsh Folk Museum

We end discussing the tyddynnwr's life with R. Alun Roberts' observations in his lecture 'Y Tyddynnwr-Chwarelwr yn Nyffryn Nantlle'. His two grandfathers were tyddynwyr, William Thomas, Glan Gors, Tanrallt and Owen Roberts, Bryn Ffynnon, Rhosgadfan, who was Kate Roberts' grandfather as well.

To us who were tied to our own tyddynnod for the greater part of the year, our special love was our hearths and lives and the home's agricultural circle mattered most by far . . .

The quarry was something distant and peripheral somehow, with the tyddyn close to us and always enveloping us in endearment . . .

But good neighbourliness thrived well at the same time, with regular opportunities for people to offer a favour and lend a hand to the unfortunate. Charity concerts were arranged for those who'd lost a cow or other unfortunate occasions, and there was an open hand on occasions such as weddings to start a home. Loyalty and monetary favours, especially as offerings on death, with blood relationship counted a lot especially in difficult times. And the care of the young for the wellbeing of the aged was a responsibility accepted without question . . .

The good wife on the tyddyn handling the butter and eggs and exchanging them in the village shop for goods, such as sugar and tea and meat, and at that time baking her own bread and queen of her hearth . . .

Tyddyn life was life close to nature, with no regular daily contact with the village. The turn of the seasons, more than almanac days denoted the days, even though an almanac was at hand on the hearth, with spring's greenness and autumn's yellow page apparent and relevant . . .

By the house, the sheep pen and churn pool, and garden. Early potatoes were grown there, gooseberries and black currants and permanent plants like horseradish and wormwood and camomile, but in the potato field, annual crops such as carrots, swedes, beans and turnips. The fact was there was not much effort put into the gardens but for the wife's small garden by the door where favourite flowers and medicinal herbs were grown, because the tyddynnwr-quarryman's delight was stock of all kinds – mountain pony or two or sheepdog or terrier – stock and not crop, because he was, as the 'bare-house' man, in the shepherding tradition from the beginning. It is just as difficult to take a man from his family.

The Villages

With the quarries continuing to expand and the need for more workers increasing, people continued to move into the locality. Second and third generations were living and working there by now, with an urgent need for more homes for everybody. The time came when there was no more suitable land for tyddynnod available. The next step therefore was to build 'tai moel', houses with no land attached, building them as a rule by the existing tracks, and that is how the quarrying villages came into being. Rhostryfan, Rhosgadfan, Carmel and Fron villages developed during the second half of the nineteenth century, on land that was previously part of Uwchgwyrfai common fifty years earlier. The villages are clusters of houses encircled by tyddynnod, and on relatively high ground. Usually the tyddynwyr would be prepared to sell plots of land to build houses on them; for example, by 1890 Bryn Gwynedd and Bryn Gwyrfai were built on one of Cae'r Gors' fields. There were existing small villages around the parish churches in Llanwnda, Llandwrog and Llanllyfni but the rest of Dyffryn Nantlle's villages came into being as a direct result of the growth of the slate industry in the nineteenth century, where there were no villages at all except for a few houses in some places such as Nantlle. Other villages were built nearby, outside our study area, Groeslon, Penygroes, Talysarn, Nebo, Nantlle, Tanrallt, and Llanllyfni expanded as well.

Rhosgadfan lies facing the sea on the N.W. slope of Moeltryfan, at a height of 230-280 m. and within easy reach of Moeltryfan and Cors-y Bryniau quarries the opposite side of the mountain. Rhostryfan is barely a mile downhill from Rhosgadfan, at a height of 140-170m., further from the quarries, but amongst the earliest tyddynnod and old hafotai. The two villages were built after 1850 on common land, industrial villages with numerous shops, chapels, a school, and rows of terraced houses. The houses are quite plain, cheaply built on the whole, and not half as attractive architecturally as the estate village of Llandwrog.

Carmel's site at a height of 220 – 270m.on the N.W. slope of Mynydd y Cilgwyn is similar, once again convenient for Cilgwyn and Penyrorsedd quarries on the other side of the mountain, and others near Fron. We have cluster of houses again with long terraces, on the road up the parish towards the common and on the cross road, directly above the old mountain wall.

The hamlet of Cilgwyn is even nearer the quarries, within a few minutes' walk to Cilgwyn Quarry and within reach of valley floor quarries such as Dorothea and Talysarn. Scattered tyddynnod, a few houses and a chapel, that's all there is.

Y Fron is situated between Moeltryfan, Cilgwyn and Mynydd Mawr mountains, near the quarries already mentioned and within a stone's throw of Fron and Braich quarries. Developed from the mid-nineteenth century as two strips along the road towards Penyrorsedd and beside the railroad to Fron Quarry, with two chapels and shops at one time. The village had several names: Cesarea after the chapel, Upper Llandwrog or Llandwrog Uchaf denoting its site within the parish, Bron-y-foel, on Moeltryfan's shoulder, and the present name, Y Fron.

The villages were built within a short period of about fifty years, coinciding with the main growth of the slate industry. They must have been very lively, busy places, with houses appearing like mushrooms, and people moving in continuously. The chapels were built at the same time, which explains why so many slate villages have Biblical names, adopting one of the chapels' names: Carmel, Cesarea, Nebo, Nasareth, Ebeneser (Deiniolen later), and Bethesda. Because the tyddynnod were there before the villages names were given for clusters of them, some of which are still in use:

Rhosgadfan – Hen Gapel, Pen-ffridd, Pen-ffordd and Rhosgadfan (the earliest tyddyn)
Rhostryfan – Caeau Cochion, Rhos-isaf
Waunfawr – Bryn Pistyll, Bryn Eithin, Hafod Olau, Pentre Waun, Ty'n Gerddi.

The site was determined by its proximity to the quarries and where fairly level ground was available. Space had to be left around the quarries for possible future expansion, and so they were built on the opposite side of the mountain, on land more exposed to the elements, facing winds from the sea, but with magnificent views.

I am seven and a half years old, sitting on the roadside by the gate. There is a large flat stone there, and that is where I sit nursing my younger brother, Dafydd, in a shawl. It's a fine day. In front of me is Anglesey and Afon Menai, the Irish Sea extending to the horizon, Caernarfon castle with its nose reaching out to the river and the town a small body behind. Small, white-sailed boats go through the bar, and Niwbwrch sands and the Foryd gleam like a colt's back in the sun. Nobody moves along the road, it's perfectly quiet.

Y Lôn Wen, Kate Roberts

The little villages with their numerous chapels and shops grew on the mountains' edges, and when the penny post came in 1840 with a need for an acceptable name for every locality, what was done was to adopt the name of the strongest Non-conformist chapel, and that is how villages such as Carmel, Cesarea, Nebo and Nasareth got their names and how we lost hold of many picturesque names to many places that had noticeably bare names after the choice!

R. Alun Roberts

The names for localities before the villages came into being could have been kept e.g. Nebo – Mynydd Llanllyfni, Carmel – Bryn Melyn, Cesarea – Bron-y-foel.

They have been, perhaps, the most important legacy of the Industrial Revolution in Caernarvonshire, for they created an entirely new type of social community, with a vigorous culture and sturdy independence unsuspected by those who see only the drab exterior.

A History of Caernarvonshire, A.H. Dodd

That is how an industrial region developed with many villages close to each other, some relatively small, others larger, rather than one large town. A similar pattern more or less can be seen in the other slate regions. As a result of the industrial economy the villages had a greater scope of amenities and services compared with other villages in agricultural regions. For example, the following services were available in Talysarn in 1886:

Types of merchants and other services in 1886

butcher 4	confectioner 1	greengrocer 3
chemist 1	smith 3	clothes shop 5
grocer 14	flour merchant 1	coal merchant 4
ironmonger 2	carpenter 1	doctor 2
bookseller 1	police station 1	post office 1
bakery 1	train station 1	innkeeper 2
school 1	tailor 4	vicar 1
preacher 1	accountant 1	painter 1
newsagents 1	insurance agent 2	haulier 1

The poor picture drawn of the quarry society has already been mentioned, but it was not so during the late nineteenth century. The industry was growing, and the multitude of services in the villages shows that the economy was lively. Harder times came with the 1914-18 World War, the 1920s depression and the 1939-45 War, but the quarry community enjoyed a fairly prosperous period prior to that. The quarrymen looked down their noses at the hordes that came from Môn to the quarries: 'they were looked upon as starving uncivilised people teeming to the quarries for food. To the quarryman, they were inferior people.' ('Y Chwarelwr a'i Gymdeithas yn y Bedwaredd Ganrif a'r Bymtheg,' *Cof Cenedl,* R. Merfyn Jones.)

Work in the quarries was unsettled during the first half of the twentieth century. Though there were many quarries within the valley, and though it was possible to move to a nearby quarry when put out of work, nevertheless circumstances could be difficult when the slate market was generally weak, as it was during the 1920s. Here is an example of the unsettled state of affairs:

The Amalgamated Slate Assocn. Limited Caernarvon
The Alexandra & Moeltryfan Slate Quarries
Rhosgadfan
Llanwnda, Nth. Wales
26th July 1929

To whom it may concern,

This is to certify that Mr. William Williams of Glanrafon Hen,
Rhosgadfan, has been in our employ for the last three years.

We are sorry to part with him but at present we must do away with
some men owing to the depression in the slate trade. This is done by
giving preference to married men.

He has pleased us in every way, being an energetical worker,
always obedient and honest, and has always obeyed the rules of the
works by being punctual etc.

Wishing him every luck in the future
Griffith Griffiths
Works Manager

William was twenty-nine years old at that time, one of Glanrafon
Hen's sons, and a single man and so one of those given 'notice' to
leave. He later worked at Penyrorsedd and after marrying went to
Terfyn to live, where his sons Arwel and Cedric were brought up.

Nobody can maintain that the villages are attractive in appearance.
Cheap, plain houses were built, with numerous terraces, and many
were in a poor state, as were many tyddynnod. The poor housing, lack
of clean water and dietary deficiencies contributed to many illnesses
such as typhoid and tuberculosis. Not everybody ate healthily as has
been said of some tyddynwyr:

> The doctors complained not only of a surfeit of tea but of the
> general standard of the quarrymen's food, too much bread and
> butter and not enough healthy vegetables.
>
> R. Merfyn Jones

Even though the authorities often blamed the diet and housing for the
poor state of health among quarry families, that was not the main

cause, but rather working conditions. The main enemy surely was slate dust that caused silicosis.

In later times, at the beginning of the 1930s, Dr T.W. Wade made a survey on behalf of the Welsh Health Board, of the high incidence of deaths caused by tuberculosis amongst Gwyrfai quarrymen. This is part of his testimony:

> Many of the houses have no through ventilation . . . Again, the dwellings which are built frequently have their back walls almost in contact with the perpendicular mountainside, while what would appear to be suitable sites for houses seem to have been overlooked in favour of sheltered situations on low-lying, damp land. Indeed, in some parts the houses are such as one would expect to see in the slum parts of a city. The houses are for the most part solidly built, but few are provided with dampcourses and damp walls are common.
>
> Houses were visited in which there was no lavatory accommodation whatsoever. In some cases such dwellings were the homes of tuberculosis patients . . . Fields, waste grounds near the house, and the banks of a stream were often used for dumping the waste matter.
>
> The diet, although usually sufficient in quantity, is often improper. Tea is still consumed to great excess and is partaken of at practically every meal. In recent years another evil has been added in the shape of tinned foods. Fresh meat is not eaten to any great extent, and is not obtainable in many parts of the district until the end of the week. There is a definite lack of fresh green vegetables in the dietary. It would be expected that in a rural area such as this, where ample land is available, no deficiency of this nature would be possible. Few of the houses, however, have cultivated kitchen gardens, and little is grown except potatoes.
>
> The tendency of the people to congregate in ill-ventilated, overcrowded rooms has often been cited as a cause of illhealth, for opportunities for infection are numerous. There is a natural fatalism among Celtic people . . .

Compare the doctor's opinion with that of Lisi Jones and Kate Roberts who describe the healthy food they ate as children and you can see a contrasting point of view.

There were certainly deficiencies in many houses though, and that is one reason why Gwyrfai Rural District Council decided to erect council houses in the quarry villages towards the end of the 1930s. You can see them in Llanllechid, Bethesda, Dinorwig, Deiniolen, and in our area. They were not by any means luxurious houses but as a child I was perfectly content living in Maes Hyfryd, Carmel.

Carmel was quite self-sufficient during my childhood in the 1940s and 1950s. The world was much more confined than today, but still we were content with our lot. Mother would shop for all our food in the village, with a choice of grocers, three bakeries and a butcher. A delicacy from Caernarfon was something rare. You could chose between two cobblers to mend your shoes, buy anything under the sun at Wenallt Ironmonger's and clothes at the Post. My father never owned a car, he cycled to work in the quarry and it was on his bike that we went to see Cesarea Rovers and Mountain Rangers playing football. Father went to choir practise and Parish Council, mother to the literary society and ladies' meeting, and all of us to chapel. Sometimes I would accompany father on his rounds of the public footpaths or to visit family in Talysarn on a summer's evening. We rarely ventured further than Penygroes or Caernarfon, apart from the bus journeys to the local 'Cymanfa' (Assembly) and Cymanfa Llŷn ac Eifionydd; or on the long-awaited Sunday School trip to Rhyl, Llandudno or Colwyn Bay; or on the summer holiday trip on the Whiteways bus, to such exotic places as 'The Circular Tour of Aberglaslyn' with its magical forested landscape in contrast to Carmel's barrenness for the rest of the year.

Some village buildings have also been listed by Cadw, being typical examples of the area's vernacular architecture:

Gorphwysfa, Rhosgadfan – detached house
Tegfan and Tŷ Crwn – two single chimney houses
Tan-y-ffynnon and The Haven, Rhos Isaf – cottages
Bethel chapel and two adjoining houses, Bethel House and Rhoslwyn, Rhos Isaf.

The main use of the common during this period was for grazing. The villagers and tyddynwyr would occasionally go for a walk in summer, and to pick bilberries in season, but leisure use was very limited. The quarrymen and their families scarcely had the time nor energy left for leisure activities after their labours.

This unique landscape remains even though the quarries' time is all but over. The network of tyddynnod, grey stone walls enclosing little fields, the paths criss-crossing between tyddyn and quarry and chapel and village, and the plain villages all remind us of life in a past age.

The Graziers

One result of the slate industry's decline was the virtual ending of the quarryman-tyddynwr's way of life, which led to a change in the use made of the common by the graziers. The rest of the hill farming community with grazing rights also contributed to the drastic changes in farming during the last half century. It's evident that hill farming is in crisis these days, and so the future agricultural use of the common is uncertain.

No other significant industry replaced slate quarrying, and over the last forty years low incomes and lack of employment has been prevalent in the area. The local economy's weakness and competition from supermarkets and all things big led to a significant decrease in the villages' services and many shops had to close. There is presently no Post Office in Rhostryfan, no shop in Fron or Rhosgdafan. There is a long tradition of hill farming locally but it does not contribute much to the local economy. Over the last twenty years the number of agricultural holdings supporting a family has fallen significantly, as well as the number of workers on them.

A clear deterioration can be seen on tyddynnod land. Many are in ruins, others second homes, others housing incomers who do not use the land, and one of the main uses is for horse grazing.

Tŷ haf

Tlodi balch a wyngalchwyd – yn fodern,
A gwyn fyd a gollwyd:
Er graen lliw mae'r gorau'n llwyd,
Gwŷr Eingl sydd dan y gronglwyd.

Tim Ymryson Powys

Proud poverty is whitewashed – modernised
And the blessed world lost;
Though the gloss of colour the best is grey,
English men are under the roof.

The *Uwchgwyrfai Common Land Foundation Study* was commissioned by CYMAD in March 2000 to ascertain the common's condition as a result of grazing. Of the twenty areas studied, 6 had light grazing, medium in 12, and only 3 showed evidence of over-grazing. This was mainly on Moeltryfan, but on the whole the results augured well both agriculturally and ecologically. The present grazing should preserve the bio-diversity. Covering the whole common with heather is not desirable; the graziers want a greater percentage in pasture, and so a compromise is needed. Keeping heathery tracts would benefit the Tir Gofal scheme and shepherding is needed where over-grazing occurs.

Several monetary factors work against the farmer. The Net Income was down substantially between 1996 and 2000. The farmers are over-dependent on various schemes and sheep and cattle prices have fallen. The Sheep Annual premium, the main source of income, has also fallen.

According to the graziers there are fewer sheep on the common now compared with fifteen years ago, even though it is said that one farmer from Môn brings between 600 and 700 ewes and lambs there in spring. The common has grazing rights for 21024 sheep, an unreasonably high figure; there wouldn't be a blade of grass left! According to the general rule of 6 sheep (including lambs)/ hectare, the total number would be 6070, and the present numbers do not constitute a problem.

There are some problems however, such as sheep wandering down to the villages, and no proper management plan until 2001.

The report states that a management plan is necessary, including grants to ensure future agricultural use of the common, conservation to meet environmental needs, safeguarding farming in areas of environmental constraints, and support for farmers to adopt sustainable methods.

Society and Culture

The populace's civilised culture – raised them,
　Men of strong hearts,
　The plain kitchen college made
　Them wise though short on education.

God's Book lit their learning – an enchanting
　Unmixed inspiration;
　His Word they knew well
　And full of respect in their midst.

Y Chwarelwr, Lisi Jones

A distinct society and culture developed in the slate quarrying areas. A cliché I know, but true, as I can vouch from my experience from the late 1940s on. Several elements contributed: that many men worked together in the quarries; that the tyddynnwyr depended on each other for good turns during busy periods such as shearing and haymaking; that the villages rose like mushrooms; all together a means to create a close-knit, neighbourly society.

Non-conformism was a strong influence, with the chapels heavily involved in religious and social life. Though short of formal education, many quarrymen were self-educated, cultured, widely read, and active in various societies. All kinds of activities flourished, among them literary societies, WEA night classes, choirs and parties, eisteddfodau, brass bands, drama societies, sheepdog trials and football teams. Like many others I fondly remember Eisteddfod Mynydd y Cilgwyn, Eisteddfod Moeltryfan, Cylchwyl Lenyddol Rhostryfan, Band Moeltryfan, Côr Mynydd y Cilgwyn, Cesarea Rovers and Mountain Rangers.

Eminent writers such as T.Rowland Hughes, Caradog Prichard and Kate Roberts depicted this society in their novels and short stories, with several characteristics coming to light:

A plain, simple populace, principled, Non-conformist, radical, having 'good' values, full of Welsh culture at its best, and belonging to a sincere society, easy to understand, worth imitating.

Y deryn nos a'i deithiau,' *Cof Cenedl 3*, Dafydd Roberts

This is what O.M.Edwards saw on his walk up to Cilgwyn:

> I was gaining height rapidly on the steep road, and before long a crowd of quarrymen on their way home from work came towards me. It was pleasant to see their knowledgeable faces: and I was glad to notice, with some haggard exceptions, that they were healthy.

The strong non-conformist influence can be confirmed by the number of chapels in every village. This is the present situation, reflecting the general trend:

Rhostryfan and Rhos Isaf:
    Horeb MC 1866 – demolished, vestry the chapel
    Tabernacl A 1866 – demolished, three houses built on site 2002
    Bethel W 1836 – open occasionally
    Libanus – adapted into a house

Rhosgadfan:
    Rhosgadfan MC 1876 – closed.
    Vestry closed 2003, members joined Horeb, Rhostryfan
    Hermon A 1862-1996 – demolished
    Gorphwysfa A 1903 – open occasionally

Y Fron:
    Cesarea MC 1880 – for sale
    Bwlch-y-llyn A 1907 – being adapted into a house

Carmel:
    Carmel MC 1871 – demolished, new chapel and house built on site 1998
    Pisgah1877 – adapted into houses 2003, vestry used
    Pisgah B 1820 – St. John the Baptist Monastery
    Cilgwyn A 1877 – a retreat connected to the monastery – being converted into a house 2005
    Bryn MC 1906 – adapted into a house

Hen gapel (Old Chapel)

Emyn na chri gweddïau – ni ddaw mwy
  Oddi mewn i'w furiau,
A'r drws lle rhoed yr iasau
I'n tadau gynt wedi'i gau.

H. Meirion Huws

Hymn nor sound of prayers – will come no more
  Within its walls,
And the door wherein thrills were given
To our forefathers is closed.

It is of interest to note that there is no pub in any of the above villages, though Rhosgadfan has the Mountain Rangers Social Club, but that is a relatively recent development, and there were numerous objections to it at the time. It was an inter-dependent society, where everybody depended on good turns in the end:

I believe that my old locality's quarrymen were very dependent on each other. We lived on kindness. The tyddynnwr with a cart would lend it to one that had none to haymake and spread manure. A quarryman would lose half a day's wages to help another with the haymaking. Lose half a day to go to a neighbour's burial. Organise a concert or lecture for a man who'd lost an animal or through long illness. These people came from other areas to poor quality virgin soil. They were used to better land previously. Therefore they had to depend a lot on each other. We do not get kindness without a need for it.

Something else that's often said is that the chapel was the community centre in days gone by . . . It is true that we saw each other in chapel, but not everybody socialised there . . . Everybody went home alone after the sermon, apart from the young people. Meetings were held such as literary societies, reading meetings, and children's meetings in mid-week, but it was the young who attended these. The grown ups went to the prayer meeting and society. The social life was in the homes. People wouldn't visit each

103

other every night, but it was customary for a neighbour to drop in quite often and to stay late sometimes.

If a neighbour came in he would join us for this meal (supper). The evening would be spent like this talking, and nine times out of ten it would be story telling.

Y Lôn Wen, Kate Roberts

Do you agree with Kate Roberts that you must have a need before there are kindnesses? Do our relationships with each other suffer because of our life of ease? Some can see the need better than others, surely.

But don't believe that all quarrymen were saints! As in Kate Roberts' description of Winni Ffinni Hadog's family in *Te yn y Grug*, and the terrible tales we read in *Un Nos Olau Leuad*, Caradog Prichard, there were enough 'ciaridyms', riff-raff, to be found. There was plenty of drinking, fighting, adultery and many other doubtful traits amongst some. If the villages near the common were bereft of inns, you could walk to 'Pen-Nionyn' in Groeslon, the 'Goat' and 'Mount Pleasant' in Llanwnda or the 'Newborough' in Bontnewydd, with plenty of choice in Penygroes or Caernarfon, and the paths to the wells were welltrodden. Not that I'm suggesting for a moment that frequenting taverns is a sin!

It is evident that there was another side to the society in Dafydd Roberts' interesting article, previously quoted:

Maybe we were too ready to accept our history and stories about these localities from the mouths of those trained to speak in public and to record knowledgeably by chapel and Big Pew. This area of Gwynedd was not a black and white society of sinners and saved, but rather a society where chapel and tavern frequenters mingled, united in the quarrying experience. The daily tasks there put its stamp on community and society, and that is the unified experience that joined the teetotaller and drunkard.

'*Y deryn nos a'i deithiau*', *Cof Cenedl 3*, Dafydd Roberts

This viewpoint is supported by Thomas Parry:

> Everybody thinks of this society as a narrow Puritan one . . . It was Puritan in the sense that some types of behaviour were prohibited. But that was the ideal. Practically there wasn't much difference between that age and our loose one. There were bastard children then, and gunshot weddings. John Jones, Tyn-y-gadlas, one of the most inspired at public praying in Carmel chapel, would call openly at 'Pen-nionyn' for his pint of beer . . . The true difference is that that age had standards, even though it did not attain them all the time, while our age tends to be without any standards at all.
>
> *Amryw Bethau*, Thomas Parry

Many who became eminent in the literary world were brought up in this locality. I suppose that it could be construed as bragging by one of the natives, but hardly anywhere else can compare with Dyffryn Nantlle in this respect. The academics Sir Thomas Parry and Dr. Dafydd Glyn Jones and the gifted writer Gruffudd Parry from Carmel; the poet Lisi Jones from Fron; one of our best dramatists, Dr. John Gwilym Jones, from Groeslon; Gwilym R. Jones, Idwal Jones, R.Williams Parry from Talysarn; Mathonwy Hughes, R.Alun Roberts, Silyn Roberts from the Cymffyrch slopes; Dic Tryfan and his short stories from Rhosgadfan and many more.

But the most important literary figure directly connected with the Uwchgwyrfai common locality is without doubt Kate Roberts, who is accepted as the mistress of the short story in Welsh, and a remarkable novelist, as well as being a literary critic of note and an inspiration to many other writers. As previously stated, she was brought up on Cae'r Gors tyddyn, and her upbringing along with her experiences between her birth in 1891 and leaving for college in 1910 and subsequent visits home to see her parents, the environmental and human influences of Rhosgadfan, all forming a rich well for some of the best literature in the Welsh Language. The common and neighbouring area, and the tyddynwyr and villagers' lives are described in detail in such books as *O Gors y Bryniau, Deian a Loli, Laura Jones, Rhigolau Bywyd, Traed Mewn Cyffion, Te yn y Grug,* and *Y Lôn Wen.* Two have been adapted for television, *Te yn y Grug* and *Traed Mewn Cyffion,* where the common and tyddynnod form a perfect background for filming. The gorse and heather colours, Moel

Smytho's silence, the detailed accounts of various environmental aspects are recurring themes in her work. It is with her words in the main that I've tried to bring this story to life.

Economic and Social Changes

I've tried to condense the social and economic changes since 1750:

a) From 1750 to 1900
Great economic and social changes occurred during this period, especially during the nineteenth century, causing changes on the common and the use made of it. Parts of the common disappeared with the spread of the slate pits and huge rubble tips. Tyddynnod were built on the common, gradually encroaching up the slopes, followed by a rapid increase in population, which saw the building of villages, also on what was once common land. We had a settled population with plenty of work locally. The tyddynnod and villages were situated within easy reach of the quarries, and a pattern of paths emerged connecting tyddynnod, village, quarries and chapels to each other. The common became more intensely grazed because there were many more tyddynnod than the old hafotai. A railway was opened in 1877, the Bryngwyn Branch of the Welsh Highland Railway, to enable the transport of slate to Caernarfon.

b) From 1900 to 1970
As a result of the slate industry's decline the population decreased because of lack of employment. Since there was not much agricultural value to the tyddynnod by now, and since they lacked the vital services, water, sewerage and electricity, many moved into the villages. Men had to travel further to work, in factories like Bernard Wardle and Ferodo in Caernarfon, or even out of Wales to places like Rugby, Coventry and Crosby in the 1950s.
The Welsh Highland railway closed in 1937.

c) From 1970 to the present
By today a number of tyddynnod on the common's boundary are ruins, others second homes, and a number of incomers from England, many retired, have come to live on the tyddynnod and in the villages. Unemployment is still a problem and young people are leaving the area. The villages have lost many services as well.

Very few tyddynnod remain a 'tyddyn' in the traditional sense of the word today. About half a dozen keep sheep, chickens and some goats, others belong to incomers who have fled the cities to enjoy quiet rural lives.

The soil's condition has deteriorated on many of the tyddynnod's fields, gradually merging into mountain pasture again, and the paths are used for leisure only. Social changes mean we have more leisure time by now.

The graziers have not managed the common as efficiently either. Some bring their sheep from afar to graze over summer, without a sense of hefting. Some of these factors' effects are evident in the following statistics for the three parishes containing parts of the common.

Some population details from the 1991 Census (Gwynedd Council)

	Llanwnda	Llandwrog	Betws Garmon
Total inhabitants 1981	1715	2391	319
Total inhabitants 1991	1855	2456	257
% under 16	22	18	16
% of houses with O.A.P.s only	28	27	19
% of incomers	5	6	7
% 3 + speaking Welsh	81	78	56

Mathonwy Hughes was brought up on Brynllidiart tyddyn above Tanrallt in Dyffryn Nantlle, a stone's throw from our area of study, and these changes are crystallised in two essays by him in his book, *Atgofion Mab y Mynydd.*

'Creu Tyddyn' Creating a Tyddyn

In the beginning there was mountain. Only bare mountain. The place was a lonely cwm and nothing else.

Hundreds of times I imagined what kind of man was the old brother who first dreamt he could create a bit of tyddyn in such a place. I imagined seeing him, bearded creature, bowed on climbing the slopes in his woollen shirtsleeves, pick and spade on his shoulders. Standing for a moment, a look around before spitting on his palms and getting on with it. Picking and digging, digging and picking. Coming across a rather large stone. Avoiding it. Must bring a sledgehammer for this tomorrow . . . Tomorrow and two days hence and three days hence the old brother will be there at dawn. He keeps at it from day to day, month to month and from year to year in rain and fair weather, in the grip of cold winds and under a strong sun till he has by now a field or two to his name and a better pasture in the bargain. That's how Brynllidiart came into being, an oasis of tyddyn on the highland's shoulder . . .

I heard that the place was but 'three acres and a cow' of tyddyn when my grandfather rented it as a robust young man before getting married . . .

With the pittance of a quarry wage and unremitting labour and his wife's thriftiness he succeeded to scrape a living and raise a family. Digging and more digging was his lot also till he managed to put two pennies together to get a wooden plough and pony and cart. Things began to shift afterwards. Many a time I heard my mother relate how it was her father with his little pony who had created hayfields on the mountainous tyddyn I was born and brought up on.

Before the old man shut his eyes on the world and his life's labour, the tyddyn was fourteen acres of good grass, apart from the mountain pasture and bog that encircled it. The place held about five milking cows and heifers and the occasional rearing calf and sixty or more sheep.

'Dim ar ôl' Nothing left

Nobody went to live in the old home after us. Who would venture to live in such a remote place ever again? Time was the only tenant to claim Brynllidiart.

A while ago, after all those years, I went up on my own, taking my time to have one look at the old mountains and to breathe a lungful of the mountain's fresh air. Even the path we used to walk (and run along) on our way to chapel and village had disappeared under bracken and briers. Rampant overgrowth had got the upper hand on everything.

After reaching high ground, the bogs between me and my old home had become swamps. It was only after rounding a great deal that I managed to reach the old tyddyn's land and that through a gap in a wall that never had any gaps in.

Walking hesitantly towards the spot where the old house used to stand on and finding that only bare walls remained, and one of the four walls already a cairn to nettles and dock. The cowshed was also a cairn and there was nothing to suggest a yard or hay enclosure either but vague traces. It was evident the place had been a ruin for some time. The thorn hedge had overgrown and looked frightening. There was no trace of the clear water ditch, it had long dried and grown a tough, rushy skin.

Staying around for a while afterwards and finding the whole place had turned into rough mountain pasture, with an occasional sheep pretending to graze a better piece of grass. I could not believe that such a place, which was by now nothing but a wilderness of tough, rough-grass, was hayfields at one time.

Yes, the mountain had recovered its property. The two ends of the circle had met and merged into one again.

Use of the Common

a) From 1750 to 1970

Industrial – the quarries

Agricultural – Very similar to the pre-1750 period, but with more intensive grazing because of the large number of tyddynnod with grazing rights. Quite responsible management of the common by the tyddynwyr and for their own good they secured good pasture, did not keep too many sheep, which would result in overgrazing, burned heather and practiced hefting. There was a shift from keeping mainly cattle to mainly sheep with a few ponies also seen. Peat was still raised until coal came to be readily available.

Settlements – People lived here, on the tyddynnod, as people had lived here during the Iron Age.

Leisure – There would be some walking on the common, but very little because there was not much leisure time till the second half of the twentieth century, only the occasional picnic and a bit of bilberry picking in season. Some walkers went up Mynydd Mawr. It was only during the last quarter of a century that the paths became prominent.

After people moved here to live, many children lived within easy reach of the common and they went there to play. Yet again we turn to Kate Roberts for evidence and for her descriptions of the wildlife seen on the common.

> It was sheer pleasure for us to take a walk on the mountain as we did on a summer's day. Discovering for the first time that plant, 'corn carw', stag's horn moss, and pulling its stubborn twists from heather bases, hoping to obtain yards of it. Then picking crowberry, the small, bitter-tasting bilberries that grew among the heather. It took ages to obtain enough of them for a tart, but that tart would be much better than a bilberry tart. The boys would search for lapwings' nests, and fish in the streams, and I never tasted any trout to compare with the trout my brothers caught in Penbryn's little stream. A narrow road called Lôn Wen ran through the middle of this moorland, because of the white rock in its soil.

Y Lôn Wen, Kate Roberts

We can't discuss children playing without referring to *Te yn y Grug*, where we have Begw, Mair and Winni Ffinni Hadog's adventures wandering the slopes. Here is a taster:

Just before turning onto the mountain, whom did they see on the road but Winni Ffinni Hadog, standing arms outstretched as if doing drill.

'You shan't pass', she challenged.

The other two girls tried to escape past her, but Winni's two arms came down like a wooden soldier's and then she took hold of both's free hands and turned them around.

'I'm coming with you to the mountain,' she said.

'Who said you could come?' Mair asked.

'How do you know we're going to the mountain', said Begw.

'If you knew me, you wouldn't ask such questions,' Winni replied.

'Is it true you're a witch?' asked Begw.

'A little girl like you shouldn't ask questions.'

Te yn y Grug, Kate Roberts

The roads then were also safe enough for us to play on them, playing ball, skipping, quoits, marbles and a 'small house' on the bank on the river's opposite side. But we had to get the assistance of two trees behind the enclosure to play swings, and find a barrel to play seesaw.

Atgofion, Kate Roberets

And Carmel in the early twentieth century:

But there's another sound on the crystal air tonight. A sound as if wooden wheels without hoops on them were being driven on hard pavements, rising and striking in their speed. The sound comes from the 'mynydd bach' (small mountain) – a patch of common below Rhes Ffrynt – and the sound of voices mixed in it – voices like people talking in the night. They're skating and I've got to go over and have a look.

There's a long snake of a slide, raised on a slope on the common, with somebody farsighted having carried water when it started to freeze about five o'clock, pouring it over it till you can move along like soap on glass . . .

It was an important enough evening to meet the men coming home from the quarry. There was no need to go far that evening. The sound of the Dorothea men's footsteps could be heard from near Tŷ Mawr, and so I might as well wait there in case the disappointment if there was no hoop might be two-sided . . . Yes, it had come safely over the shoulder, a brand new hoop.

Learning to roll a hoop entailed perseverance to develop discipline and craft. That hoop was unblemished two yards of threequarter iron rod turned into a perfect circle, and the welding so fine that no critical eye could see it once the fire's trace had withered. And a hook had come with it also. This was of narrower material, turned into a U shape at one end, and the U then turned back on itself till it was square on to the length and comfortably loose on the hoop, and the holding end turned into a link to enable it to be hung on a nail in the coalshed.

It will take some practicing to learn exactly where on the hoop to place the hook to steer it and keep it going; to come to know at what speed one needs to turn the hook to make a brake instead of driving, and the day will come, in the distant future, when the driver will know within a yard to the back door where it's neccessary to lift it shining like a shilling and still turning on its own power. And nobody will have a hope of saying where the splice is by then . . .

A piece of yellow calico was best for making a marbles bag, but because a string was needed to close its mouth safely it was no work for an apprentice, but for an experienced needlewoman or tailor. There was another purpose for the string as the braces' strap could be put through to make it hang on the thigh like a knight's sword while the tournament went ahead.

They were long, golden evenings, Dinas Dinlle's sea blue, and June breezes waving the hay fields. It's dry enough to play marbles on the bank by Llidiart y Mynydd, and since it's going to be playing for keeps and not lending, the arrangements have to be perfectly correct. A ring any old how by guesswork won't do. One must have a piece of string with two sticks tied to each end. Hold one safely where the centre should be and take the other round marking carefully a perfect circle. The central mark should be left clear as this will be the target for throwing our taws at. The nearest to it will start with the other four beginning in turn according to how near the bull they were. One problem will arise, how many a head to put down. It won't be difficult to reach an understanding over four or five, but if there is a mixture of stone marbles and nut marbles, there must be an understanding how many clay marbles will be put down to correspond to one stone marble. After reaching an agreement of four a head, the laying will have to be observed carefuly, everybody in turn, and be ready to shout 'clay' if there is any doubt. The owner is sure to deny, but it will be easy to break the argument by knocking the marble against the lower teeth and listening to its sound. A stone marble tinkles while a clay one beats like wood.

'Clay mate.'

'Stone.'

'Hit it against the wall then. If it's stone it will hold but clay will break.'

'No, I'll put two then.'

'Truth to the light you see.'

There will never be any bending of the rules while playing for keeps, because the new calico bag could be emptier going home tonight, and one has a bullet as a taw. They say that a bullet is a ballbearing from a motor's engine. It shines like silver and is easy to flip with the thumb knuckle. A glass ginger-beer bottleneck won't have a chance against it – that's the effect of industrial development – but a colourful glass taw as a present from Town is another matter. And if the bag is emptier going home – well, one must accept the turns of fate. And there'll be fresh bread for supper, and the butter is yellow even though the cows are on the mountain.

Blwyddyn Bentra, Gruffudd Parry

These are some of my own reminiscences of my childhood in Carmel during the middle years of the twentieth century.

Here's the mountain gate, its still here but there's no reason for its existence by now, with the tattered fence and sheep roaming at will. You daren't leave it open ages ago. For us Carmel children . . . the gate to freedom, the door to imagination.

'Shall we go to Graig Lwyd, boys?'

'Yes, hurry up, before the Indians arrive.'

'Away boys, dyryndyryndyryndyryn . . .

Galloping over the meandering paths, slap of the thigh to spur the steed, a false step and my legs would be covered in cactus thorns. Arriving in a lather of sweat, tether the horses to graze and climb to the rock's top. On look out, eye on brow to shadow the fierce sun, seeking the enemy with eagle eye.

'They're coming, hide boys!'

Squatting, or lying prone in the rock's shadow. Croaking of crows splitting the waiting . . .

Pant yr Eira is a depression on the mountain's slope clear of gorse and heather, facing north.

Where the sun tarries longest
Where the fresh breeze is so free.

A crowd of us cramming into Siop Doris.

'Have you got some empty boxes for us, please?'
'What do you want them for lads?'
'To go sliding in Pant yr Eira.'
'That's nice, here will these do?'

Off we rush. A midsummer's evening, the grass dried pale yellow, the Eifl pale blue through the haze and the sea a still lake. Climb to the edge of the cup – sit on the box – lean back and raise your feet – a good shove from your partner – as good as the Cresta Run any day – the thrill of not having control over your body – nostrils filling with scent of gorse, heather and rough-grass – the fifties' aromatherapy.

Over the mountain to hunt tadpoles
Water in the lake and stones slippery.

To Llyn Cob, kneeling by the stream between the two pools, stick an earthworm to wriggle on a rush, tempt the stickleback from its lair under a rock. Fill a jampot with tadpoles and some watercress. Throw smooth pieces of slate to slide over the pool's surface and shatter our shadows to smithereens. I'm sure everybody cheats a bit when counting how many times they bounce. Turn for home when our shadows dissappear and when creation darkens. Who needs Sega, Mega drive, CD ROMs, borrowing videos by the dozen and live through false second-hand experiences?

Atgof, Atgof Gynt, Dewi Tomos

Children today miss tasting rich childhood experiences. One of the last days of the year 2000 was a day of clear blue sky with the land covered by a blanket of fresh snow. Six of us responsible middle-aged children went up Moeltryfan with our children's old sledge, a vivid orange survival bag and a black bin bag. The journey in itself was sheer pleasure, treading virgin snow always gives a thrill with every step. And what fun we had, exhilerating sledging and trudging back up for ages until the sun neared its bed on the Eifl. We didn't see a single child all afternoon. At least I had a childhood I can re-live.

b) From 1970 till the present

Industrial – No production of roofing slate. Clearing of tips in Cilgwyn by Celticslate
It is intended to reopen Moeltryfan and Cors y Bryniau quarry on a limited basis, mainly to extract ornamental slate.

Settlements – Far fewer living on the tyddynnod.

Agricultural – Sheep grazing predominant. Some cattle grazing re-introduced recently.

Leisure – A far greater and more varied use, by locals and visitors. Far fewer children playing on the common now compared to 30 years or more ago

Walking – Regular use is made of the common by walkers, but not in great numbers. Plenty of paths and easy access from the roads even though there is only one designated parking space, a site to remember Kate Roberts at the top of Lôn Wen. The path used the most is to Mynydd Mawr summit from the Fron side, past Llyn Ffynhonnau and up above Cwm Du. The Four Valleys Trail crosses the common, with maps available, running from Bethesda to Llanberis, Waunfawr and Penygroes.

The common's appeal to walkers is evident, variety of paths, easy access and magnificent views. Yr Wyddfa in all its splendour, Moel Eilio and Nantlle ridges as well as the coastland from Llŷn peninsula to Gogarth, and on clear evenings the Wicklow mountains in Ireland can be seen over the blue waters.

Several groups, including Cymdeithas Edward Llwyd, Clwb Crwydro Ysgol Dyffryn Nantlle, Cyfeillion Cae'r Gors and the Ramblers organise walks here.

Pony trekking – There has been an increase in pony trekking over the last ten years, mainly from two centres, Gadlys in Rhostryfan and Snowdonia Riding School in Waunfawr, with a choice of suitable routes.

Mountain races – Two local races were held, Ras Moeltryfan from Rhosgadfan for about twenty years, and Ras Mynydd Mawr from Fron since 1986. The adults race to the summit and back, with shorter races for juniors, supported by Clwb Rhedwyr Eryri. Local runners train regularly here.

Mountain biking – limited use at present

Scrambling motorbikes – Local youths to start off with, on Moeltryfan and around Cors y Bryniau Quarry's old sheds

Orienteering – The common is used by Eryri Orienteering Club for competition once or twice a year, using a recent orienteering map.

Fishing – On Llyn Ffynhonnau mainly

Diving – Braich Quarry's pit is used on weekends by divers.

Shooting – The North Wales Muzzle Loaders Association use the Moeltryfan Quarry sheds' site on weekends.

Climbing – There are good climbs on Castell Cidwm's slopes.

It is clear that a wide range of leisure activities take place, but none on a large scale.

Some of these activities could pose a problem, with erosion problems on the increase. Over the last year or so there has been a significant increase in the number of 4WD vehicles, quad bikes and scrambling motorbikes using the common, some coming from afar, even a lorry load of motorbikes, and the erosion problem on many paths, and off paths, has now reached a serious level. If these activities continue it will have a detrimental effect on the main leisure activity of walking.

With climatic changes associated with global warming, heavier rainfall over the winter months could cause the soil to be waterlogged for a greater period and increase the rate of erosion.

The Future

Aspects related to agricultural, environmental and leisure use of the common have been discussed and any future plans will have to strive to keep the balance between them. Different bodies should co-operate to promote responsible use of the common for the future.

Agriculturally, the suggestions contained in CYMAD's report could be implemented, but even then sheep grazing would not contribute much to the economy. Another option woul be to keep sheep off the common and so improve the bio-diversity. The different grasses, heathery tracts and bogs could flourish with a possible increase in some species of flora and fauna, and shrubs and trees could have a chance to grow again. What about the farmer? As has been explained, the tyddynnod were never viable units but the hill farms, the old hafotai, could seek alternative ways to earn a living. They could diversify, and what about organic farming? If the tyddynwyr could grow crops in the old days, why can't they today? Surely meeting local demand would be a step in the right direction.

Limiting the number of sheep on the common and improving the biodiversity would possibly boost the tourist industry, which could contribute more to the local economy. The area would have greater appeal to visitors and for local leisure use.

It's likely that walking will still be the main leisure activity. More use could be made of the two most popular paths, up Mynydd Mawr and the Four Valleys Path. I believe Parc Cenedlaethol Eryri could encourage more walkers to visit places like the Moel Eilio ridge, Nantlle Ridge and the common, away from the most popular honeypots. The Four Valleys Path could be joined to the North Wales Path, which runs from Prestatyn to Bangor, creating 6-7 day walks from Prestatyn to Penygroes, or 4-5 day walks from Conwy to Penygroes. With efficient marketing these could become popular walks. We have the scenery to compare favourably with any area in Britain and they could be a substantial boost to the economy. Compare them with paths such as the Dales Way, Pennine Way, West Highland Way and Offa's Dyke Path. Historic, industrial, cultural and heritage walks could be promoted.

That is Cyfeillion Cae'r Gors' intention by establishing Canolfan Treftadaeth Kate Roberts, a multi-media heritage centre that will interpret and introduce the area's rich heritage. This could have a positive effect on the use made of the common.

Walks will be offered visiting the tyddynnod, quarries and villages, with maps and pamphlets. It will be a vital step towards preserving the area's special heritage. Cae'r Gors is typical of the quarrymen's tyddyn; Kate Roberts and other writers' work will be displayed, together with an interpretation of the area's environmental importance. All this hopefully will be a means for people, especially local inhabitants, to respect and defend this special place.

The last word is given to Kate Roberts, with Owen's meditations in the novel *Traed Mewn Cyffion*.

It was a moonlit evening, and the road was grey-white under his feet. A sheep rose from its resting place every now and again on hearing his footsteps, and ran somewhere else. The streams' sound was so quiet that he imagined they were swirling and not flowing. He sat on a big rock. The village lay like a fairyland under the moon's entrancement beneath him. Here and there like black smudges were the farmhouses, with a cluster of trees sheltering the hay enclosures and houses. The moon shone on the other houses, its light reflected off the slates. The house shadows were long, and the fields looked yellow in the light. At the very bottom was a cornfield in stooks. The earth around where he sat was dark red, and Owen knew that all the land as far as his eye could see, was like that about a hundred years ago. The people responsible for turning the land green were by now lying in the parish cemetry. Some came from the bottom of the parish to cultivate mountain soil and to live on it.

And yet those work-hardened hands' toil was not visible to him. He could imagine many countries around the world, large towns with countless streets of Moel Arian slate roofed houses, and tonight the same moon that shone on Moel Arian cast its rays to slide along those roofs, in faraway countries.

He turned his gaze towards the rubble tips. Tonight it was merely a dark patch on the mountainside. The same people who were responsible for raising tyddynnod on marshland were responsible for the quarry tip as well. For a hundred years the villagers were between these two working early and late, till they became bowed before reaching middle age. Some thought they could avoid that for their children by sending them to schools and offices and shops.

His thoughts returned to his own family. They were a typical example of the locality's families, hard-working people, who'd had their share of troubles, tried to pay their way, who'd failed many a time . . .

Some Welsh words used

cadlas – hay enclosure
tŷ gwair – hay barn
cors, mawnog – peat-bog, marsh
mawn – peat
cynefin –   environmental – habitat
              human – haunt, where one belongs
              sheep – heft
cadw i'w gynefin – keep to 'cynefin', hefting
ffridd – mountain pasture, sheep walk
hafod – summer dwelling
hendre – winter dwelling, main farmstead
swper chwarel – quarry supper
tŷ/tai moel – house/houses with no adjacent land except garden
tyddyn/tyddynnod – small-holding/holdings
tyddynnwr/tyddynwyr – small-holder/holders
bwthyn – cottage

Kate Roberts' work

O Gors y Bryniau, 1925
Deian a Loli, 1927
Rhigolau Bywyd, 1929
Laura Jones, 1930
Traed Mewn Cyffion, 1936
Ffair Gaeaf, 1937
Stryd y Glep, 1949
Y Byw sy'n Cysgu, 1956
Te yn y Grug, 1959

Y Lôn Wen, 1960
Tywyll Heno, 1962
Hyn o Fyd, 1964
Tegwch y Bore, 1967
Prynu Dol, 1969
Gobaith, 1972
Yr Wylan Deg, 1976
Haul a Drycin, 1981
Atgofion; Cyfrol 1, 1972

Dau Lenor o ochr Moeltryfan Darlith Flynyddol Llyfrgell Penygroes 1968.

About her work

Kate Roberts: *Cyfrol Deyrnged*, gol. Bobi Jones, 1969
Enaid Clwyfus, John Emyr, 1976
Crefft y Llenor, John Gwilym Jones, 1977
Kate Roberts: *Bro a Bywyd*, gol. Derec Llwyd Morgan, 1981
Kate Roberts: *Ei Meddwl a'i Gwaith*, gol. Rhydwen Williams, 1983
Erthyglau ac Ysgrifau Llenyddol Kate Roberts, gol. David Jenkins

Annwyl Kate, Annwyl Saunders, gol. Dafydd Ifans 1992
Goreuon Storïau Kate Roberts, gol. Harri Prichard Jones
Kate Roberts: *Llên y Llenor*, Eigra Lewis Roberts, 1994

English translations

A Summer's Day and Other Stories, 1946
Welsh Short Stories (Old Age, Two Storms), ed. Gwyn Jones, 1956
Kate Roberts: *Writers of Wales*, Derec Llwyd Morgan (University of Wales 1974/1991)
Feet in Chains, tr. John Idris Jones (John Jones Publishing Ltd 1996/Seren 2002)
Tea in the Heather, tr. Wyn Griffith (John Jones Publishing Ltd 1997/Seren 2002)

Translations into other languages

German : Katzen auf einer Versteigerung, Wolfgang Schamoni, 2000
Dutch
Japanese

Bibliography

Cyfansoddiadau Eisteddfod Genedlaethol Cymru Caernarfon 1959
Cynefin Consultants, Uwchgwyrfai Common Land Foundation Study
Cyngor Cefn Gwlad Cymru
Davies, D. & Jones, A., *Enwau Cymraeg ar Blanhigion* (Amgueddfa Genedlaethol Cymru, 1995)
Dodd, A. H., *A History of Caernarvonshire* (Bridge Books, 1990)
Edwards, O. M., *Yn y Wlad* ac *Ysgrifau Eraill* (Hughes a'i Fab,1958)
Griffith, John, *Chwareli Dyffryn Nantlle a Chymdogaeth Moeltryfan* (1889)
Hughes, Mathonwy, *Bywyd yr Ucheldir* (Llyfrgell Sir Gaernarfon, 1973); *Atgofion Mab y Mynydd* (Gwasg Gee, 1982)
Jones, Lisi, *Dwy Aelwyd* (Cyhoeddiadau Mei, 1984); *Swper Chwarel* (Llyfrfa'r Methodistiaid Calfinaidd, 1974)
Jones, R. Merfyn, *'Y Chwarelwr a'i Gymdeithas yn y Bedwaredd ganrif ar Bymtheg'*, *Cof Cenedl 1*, Gol. G.H. Jenkins (Gomer, 1986)
Lindsay, Jean, *A History of the North Wales Slate Industry* (David & Charles, 1974)
Parry, Gruffudd, *Blwyddyn Bentra* (Llyfrgell Gwynedd, 1975): *Cofio'n Ôl* (Gwasg Gwynedd, 2000)
Parry, Thomas, *Amryw Bethau* (Gwasg Gee, 1996); *Tŷ a Thyddyn* (Llyfrgell Sir Gaernarfon, 1972)
Rhestr a Map Degwm Plwy Llanwnda 1849 (Archifdy Gwynedd)
Roberts, Dafydd, *'Y deryn nos a'i deithiau'*, Cof Cenedl 3, Gol. G. H. Jenkins (Gomer, 1988)
Roberts Kate, *Atgofion* (Tŷ ar y Graig, 1974); *O Gors y Bryniau* (Hughes a'i Fab, 1932); *Rhigolau Bywyd* (Cambrian News, 1929); *Te yn y Grug* (Gwasg Gee, 1959); *Traed Mewn Cyffion* (Gwasg Aberystwyth, 1936); *Y Lôn Wen* (Gwasg Gee, 1960)
Roberts, R. Alun, *Hafodydd Brithion* (Hugh Evans a'i feibion, 1947); *Y Tyddynnwr-Chwarelwr yn Nyffryn Nantlle* (Llyfrgell Sir Gaernarfon, 1969)
Royal Commission on Ancient Monuments
Tomos, Dewi, *Atgof, Atgof Gynt* (Cyngor Gwynedd, 1997); *Llechi Lleu* (Cyhoeddiadau Mei, 1980); *Straeon Gwydion* (Gwasg Carreg Gwalch, 1990)
Thomas, David, *Cau'r Tiroedd Comin* (Gwasg y Brython, 1952)
Wade, T. W., *Gwyrfai Rural District* (1930)
Williams, W. Gilbert, *O Foeltryfan i'r Traeth; Breision Hanes*
Ymddiriedolaeth Archaeolegol Gwynedd/Gwynedd Archaeological Trust